Cultural PROGRAMMING *for* LIBRARIES

Linking Libraries, Communities, and Culture

DEBORAH A. ROBERTSON

*With the Public Programs Office
of the American Library Association*

*With assistance from Susan Brandehoff,
Mary Davis Fournier, and Laura Hayes*

American Library Association
Chicago   2005

Composition by ALA Editions in Univers and Sabon using QuarkXPress 5.0 on a PC platform.

Printed on 50-pound white offset, a pH-neutral stock, and bound in 10-point coated cover stock by McNaughton & Gunn.

The paper used in this publication meets the minimum requirements of American National Standard for Information Sciences—Permanence of Paper for Printed Library Materials, ANSI Z39.48-1992.∞

Library of Congress Cataloging-in-Publication Data

Robertson, Deborah A.
    Cultural programming for libraries : linking libraries, communities, and culture / by Deborah A. Robertson with the Public Programs Office of the American Library Association.
       p. cm.
    Includes bibliographical references and index.
    ISBN 0-8389-3551-6 (alk. paper)
    1. Libraries—Cultural programs—United States. I. American Library Association. Public Programs Office. II. Title.
    Z716.4.R625 2005
    021.2—dc22   2005007349

Printed in the United States of America.

09   08   07   06   05   5   4   3   2   1

CONTENTS

ACKNOWLEDGMENTS

The American Library Association Public Programs Office has worked with and been inspired by countless individuals and organizations, who have in turn provided the raw material for this book. They include, but are not limited to, ALA Public Programs Office staff, past and present—Asa App, Brenda Barrera, Susan Brandehoff, Mary Davis Fournier, Pamela Goodes, Laura Hayes, Mara Karduck, Audrey Johnson, Malinda Little, Marsha Morgan, and Sofiana Peterson; intern Michelle Thurman; consultants Christine Watkins and Debra Wilcox Johnson; and the five thousand–plus librarians who have participated in PPO grant programs and initiatives.

Special thanks to the following individuals and organizations:

Andrea Anderson, Sally Anderson, Frances Ashburn, Peggy Barber, Cliff Becker, Marilyn Boria, Dianne C. Brady, Lee Briccetti, Matt Brogan, Mary Carlogmagno, Marlene Chamberlain, Pat Chester, Natalie Cole, Judith Cooper, Kathleen de la Peña McCook, Stuart Dybek, Riva Feshbach, Rich Gage, Patrick Golden, Jaimy Gordon, Tim Gunn, Ruth Hamilton, Rochelle Hartman, Marianne Hartzell, Gerald Hodges, Linda Holtslander, Barbara Immroth, Deborah Jacobs, Helen Klaviter, Marcia Kuszmaul, Mildred Larson, Sarah Ann Long, Jill McCorkle, Dwight McInvaill, Esther Mackintosh, Carolyn Margolis, Sally Mason-Robinson, Diane Wood Middlebrook, E. Ethelbert Miller, Alan Moores, Sheila Murphy, George Needham, Joseph Parisi, Jennifer Paustenbaugh, Nancy Pearl, Thomas Phelps, Susan Richards, Jim Roe, Rhea Rubin, Susan Saidenberg, Scott Russell Sanders, Michael Sartisky, Martha Sewell, Sam Silvio, Wicky Sleight, Lee Smith, Linda C. Smith, Lynn Smith, Valerie Smith, Virginia Stanley, Barbara Stauffer, Ilan Stavans, Ina Stern, Lou Storey, Victor Swenson, Judith Tennebaum, Herman Viola, Natalie Weikart, Colson Whitehead, Stuart Wilson, Kevin Young, Stephen Young, David Zeidberg.

American Library Association, Annenberg/CPB Project, Barnes and Noble, Choices for the 21st Century/Brown University, Federation of State Humanities Councils, Flossmoor (Ill.) Public Library, John S. and James L. Knight Foundation, Louisiana Endowment for the Humanities, Minnesota Children's Museum, National Endowment for the Arts, National Endowment for the Humanities, National Library of Medicine, National

Video Resources, Nextbook, *Poetry* magazine/Modern Poetry Association (Poetry Foundation), Poets House, Public Library Association, Robert Wood Johnson Foundation, Smithsonian Institution, University of Illinois Graduate School of Library and Information Science, Vermont Center for the Book, Vermont Humanities Council, and the Wallace Foundation.

Culture is the name for what people are interested in, their thoughts, their models, the books they read and the speeches they hear, their table-talk, gossip, controversies, historical sense and scientific training, the values they appreciate, the quality of life they admire. All communities have a culture. It is the climate of their civilization.

—WALTER LIPPMANN

A Life With Poetry

Meet the Author and Poet Naomi Shihab Nye

"Mother Palestine" by Suleiman Mansour. Used by permission of Simon & Schuster.

Welcome to *Cultural Programming for Libraries* and the world of cultural programming. This book is for you if you are responsible for or interested in developing and presenting programming with a cultural focus for public audiences outside the formal learning environment in any type of library—public, academic, school, or special. Maybe you have been involved in cultural programming as a spectator or participant, a member of a team planning and creating programming, the leader of a team, or the focus of a one-person show. Wherever you are in the spectrum of enhancing your library's role as a cultural center, you want to enhance your skills, increase your effectiveness, or expand your creativity. You want the tools and the inspiration. This book is designed to provide basic information for the novice, rejuvenation for the experienced programmer, and links to new possibilities for the expert.

The guidance contained here is the result of a movement that has been growing for many years—under the influence of many programs and initiatives, many organizations, and above all, many dedicated individuals—with the goal of fostering cultural programming as an integral part of library service in all types of libraries.

The emphasis on "cultural" programming encompasses the arts, sciences, and humanities and the community dialogue engendered by such events as arts performances, interpretive exhibitions, and literary book discussions. The audience for cultural programming is primarily adults as well as young adults and families, because many resources specifically for children's programming already exist.

Cultural programming in libraries has a long history and continues to evolve along with the changing needs and interests of communities. The role of cultural center and programming provider springs from the library's educational mission and parallels social and educational trends. The establishment of public libraries in the United States in the mid- to late-nineteenth century, for example, coincided with the growth of the Chautauqua movement, university extension, and the organization of clubs and societies for intellectual pursuits (as well as the establishment of the American Library Association).

Although the literary role of libraries is perhaps most visible, with book discussions and author appearances among the best-known types of programming for adults in public libraries, libraries of all types are reaching out with a variety of cultural program formats with great success. This book's purposes will be served if the bar of excellence in programming is set ever higher as librarians and library advocates center the library as a cultural hub in the communities they serve.

In the work of the American Library Association Public Programs Office (PPO), from which this book draws extensively, there is evidence of a wide range of effective programming in libraries, which is reflected in stories and examples. PPO aims to support and encourage librarians in thoughtful planning, diverse programming, engaging presenters, professional-level marketing, development of audiences beyond the library's traditional base of users, and series of programs that engage individuals in meaningful dialogue and learning.

In detailed fashion, this book provides background, practical steps, and ideas to develop the library's capacity to present excellent adult, young adult, and family cultural programming on topics, themes, and issues for a wide array of audiences across cultures. It shows library managers, staff, and volunteers how to assess community needs and interests, set goals and establish measurable outcomes, and develop partnerships that will result in high-quality, well-attended programs. Readers will learn to use programming to enhance, highlight, and drive the use of library collections and gain community visibility and support through programming.

Libraries that have participated in American Library Association–sponsored cultural programming have developed a wide variety of effective promotional materials. Examples of such materials are included as illustrations throughout the book and can serve as excellent models for local efforts.

Also addressed in this volume: fund-raising and in-kind donations for programming, the nitty-gritty of finding and hosting appropriate and skillful presenters, the ins and outs of hosting programs, and real-life examples and models of successful programming. Finally, this book highlights additional sources of many necessary programming and financial resources.

The PPO staff encourages you to make use of resources on the websites (http://www.ala.org/publicprograms and www.ala.org/publicprograms/orc/), attend programs and conferences for further professional development and networking, apply for grants offered by the office, access staff resources, and contribute your own expertise.

Good luck and good programming.

CHAPTER 1

Making the Case
for Cultural Programming

Cease not to learne until thou cease to live.
—DU FAUR, 1608

Learn young, learn fair; learn old, learn more.
—SCOTTISH PROVERB

In celebration of the exhibition and in
appreciation for the hard work and generosity
of all those who have made it possible,

Please join us for a reception
to mark the opening of
Elizabeth I: Ruler and Legend
at the Newberry Library

Friday, the third of October
two thousand and three
half after five in the evening
The Newberry Library
Towner Fellows' Lounge
60 West Walton Street
Chicago, Illinois 60610

cocktails and hors d'oeuvres
followed by a short gallery walk with the curator

R.S.V.P. by September 26 to Dina Spoerl
at 312.255.3539 or spoerld@newberry.org
Parking is available in the Newberry's lot

Making the case for cultural programming at your library is a key component in ensuring its success. You may need to convince your library administration, your board, funding agencies, or segments of the community that cultural programming and community dialogue are important, essential, and worthy of support. You will need to be able to answer such questions as: What difference will cultural programming make? Why should the library take this responsibility? Who will benefit? What is needed and why is it needed? How is the library distinctly qualified to present cultural programming? How will cultural programming address the library's goals?

The Library's Role and Mission in Learning and Society

Library mission statements generally refer in some way to continuous education or lifelong learning: aiding in education is central to the purpose of libraries of all types. In many ways, the case for cultural programming is the case for the library itself. Libraries exist for a public good. They benefit all equally. They are uniquely qualified to deliver information and to make sense of it. By selecting, collecting, organizing, preserving, and making available the material effects of culture, librarians make libraries the most viable of venues for cultural programming. Through live lectures, book and film discussions, author and artist events, traveling exhibitions, and other cultural programs, libraries foster community dialogue.

In today's online world, libraries and their buildings remain places of contact, community, and culture. Communities need places offering programs that both reflect and expand their interests. Audiences need places where they are made to feel welcome and comfortable. Writers, artists, performers, scholars, and other makers and purveyors of culture need places where they can share their work in person and also have their work collected, supported, disseminated, and interpreted. Individuals need places to bring their curiosity, questions, and aspirations.

"Libraries are many things to their communities," according to Susan Brandehoff, editor of the *Whole Person Catalog 3* (ALA/PPO 1994).

> They offer the practical information people need to improve their quality of life and to increase individual options in a complex society—information about health, education, business, child care, computers, the environment, looking for a job . . . and much more.
>
> Libraries also give their communities something less tangible, yet just as essential to a satisfying and productive life—nourishment for the spirit. Programs in the humanities and the arts that encourage people to think about ethics and values, history, art, poetry, and other cultures are integral to the library's mission. (p. 2)

Programming helps "to illuminate the experiences, beliefs, and values that unite us as human beings. They stimulate us to make connections where we noticed none before—between our ancestors and ourselves, between one culture and another, between the community and the individual," Brandehoff concludes.

"Libraries have a long connection with self-managed adult learning," according to Philip C. Candy in *Self-Direction for Lifelong Learning* (1991).

Throughout the nineteenth century, particularly in countries such as Australia, Canada, New Zealand, and the United States, the spread of literacy and the establishment of reading rooms accompanied the explosion of interest in many early forms of adult education—mechanics' institutes, literary and scientific societies, adult Sunday schools, and so on. In more recent times, the public library has become the focal point of initiatives to provide educational and self-educational opportunities to a wide range of the adult population within a lifelong learning perspective. Although many recent studies have been concerned with questions of organizational policy and institutional access, there has also been a reappraisal of the work of the librarian, changing from a custodial to a more consultative and advisory role. (pp. 191–92)

In his work calling for research into the library's role in the life of the user, Wayne A. Wiegand notes that libraries "have (1) made information accessible to millions of people on a variety of subjects; (2) provided tens of thousands of places where patrons have been able to meet formally as clubs or groups, or informally as citizens or students utilizing a civic institution and cultural agency; and (3) furnished billions of reading materials to billions of people" (2003, 2). However, Wiegand argues that library research has focused on the first activity and has not analyzed in depth the community role of the "library as a place" or the library's role in promoting reading and the social nature and act of reading. Likewise, the nature of these roles is not widely understood by the public.

Kathleen de la Peña McCook, author of *A Place at the Table: Participating in Community Building* (2000a) and other works about the role of libraries in community, writes in *Reference and User Services Quarterly* that "today the call for community building and civic renewal resounds in the literature of the policy sciences, higher education, and the popular press. Civic renewal is the movement calling for citizens to participate in the local efforts that build community" (2000b, 24).

"By participating at the outset in planning and visioning, librarians will be at the table and in a position to identify opportunities for the library and its services to provide solutions to community and campus challenges. This is not a simple task," according to de la Peña McCook (2000b, 25).

Cultural programming—and its attendant collaboration and audience building—is one way to make a place at the table for libraries and revitalize and energize their communities.

What Is Cultural Programming?

For the purposes of this work, cultural programming is defined as programs and series of programs presented by libraries that seek to entertain, enlighten, educate, and involve adult and family audiences, primarily in the disciplines of the arts, humanities, sciences, and public policy or community issues. This type of programming is designed to elicit dialogue, discussion, and consideration of ideas and issues, as well as to further independent study.

Who Is Doing Cultural Programming and Why?

A 1998 survey conducted by the ALA Public Programs Office found that nearly 86 percent of public libraries offered cultural programs for their communities (1999a, iii). Though that figure may have been accurate at that time, today almost every library in the country, including academic, school, and special libraries, offers some level of cultural programming for adult audiences. "We've created a demand for this kind of programming," according to Frannie Ashburn, director of the North Carolina Center for the Book and a longtime programmer at the state and national levels. "I'm delighted to see libraries rising to the challenge and meeting the demand with more and higher-quality programs."

Although no studies exist of academic, school, and special library involvement, about 30 percent of libraries participating in traveling exhibitions offered by the ALA Public Programs Office are academic libraries. While school and special libraries have been occasional participants, accounting for about 5 percent of overall involvement, they have not yet been targeted by PPO programs, and anecdotal information points to activity and interest in cultural programming and a need for resources among such libraries.

The 1998 survey conducted by the ALA Public Programs Office also found that 86 percent of public libraries serving populations over five thousand presented some form of cultural programming for adults, including 62 percent that offered literary book discussion programs (1999a, 1). While this probably represents increased activity, it is not a new undertaking for libraries.

A survey investigating adult services conducted more than a decade earlier, in 1986, found that 55 percent of public libraries serving communities of twenty-five thousand or more presented book talks/reviews, and 74 percent presented live programs. Varying numbers of those libraries, ranging from 5 percent to 38 percent, organized programming for special groups, with the highest percentages of programs being directed toward older adults and parents (Wallace 1990, 58–59).

Cultural programming is increasing in all types of libraries but has been perhaps most visible in public libraries. The trend has recently begun to spread among academic libraries, which are seeking ways to collaborate with other areas of the university and the community at large, as well as striving to engage the community of users and potential users in new ways.

Box 1-1 presents a sample Top 10 reasons for libraries to do cultural programming. There are many more.

Most librarians, no matter their type of institution, have recognized for some time that it is no longer sufficient or desirable for the library to be a "warehouse" for books and other materials. Today's consumers look for value added in both services and products. This value may be in the form of reference help, reader's advisory, or programs that help interpret and provide gateways to the collections. Librarians are in the ideal and enviable position to provide exactly such types of service and expertise.

In the past, the library's role as a social/cultural institution was the subject of some debate, according to Connie Van Fleet and Douglas Raber in "The Public Library as a Social/Cultural Institution" (1990). "While some argue that librarians should stick to what they know best (books),"

BOX 1-1

TOP 10 REASONS TO DO CULTURAL PROGRAMMING

10. Programming and community outreach are important roles for the library as a community center.

9. Interpretation of the collection, generally reader's advisory, is an important role for the librarian.

8. Everybody is doing it: according to surveys, an increasing number of all types of libraries are offering cultural programming.

7. It is easy to get money. Based on libraries' previous successes, local and national sources are open to funding cultural programming that makes a difference.

6. Cultural programming gains visibility for the library and its partner agencies.

5. Programming boosts circulation of materials related to the program topic—and circulation is an important measurement for libraries.

4. Programming is rewarding, enriching, and intellectually satisfying for the librarian, the audience, and the presenters.

3. Programming is something the whole family can enjoy: plan intergenerational programs, or seed a small audience with your own family members.

2. Programming fosters bonding with your coworkers: teamwork, pride, and enthusiasm develop among staff.

1. Programming is a great way to meet and network with other librarians and interesting people. (At least one librarian-scholar team met through an ALA Public Programs Office project and got married.*)

*Results may vary

say Van Fleet and Raber, "others view this restriction as an unnecessary limitation to access. This seemingly trivial argument over whether nontraditional services (generally live programming and activities) should be offered is a critical issue in the definition of the profession. Does the librarian preserve recorded knowledge to provide access to the records per se or to the knowledge and experience found within those records? Stemming from this debate is the issue of the nature of nonbook activities. Should programming be employed only as a stimulation to further use of the library's collection, or is the activity sufficient in and of itself as a means of bringing people into contact with the human record?" (458).

Van Fleet and Raber quote adult library services pioneer Margaret E. Monroe's 1981 study, which identified six functions of the library in fulfilling the cultural role:

1. To serve the arts information needs of the community (including the needs of artists and scholars)
2. To provide a showcase for the arts in the local community
3. To facilitate arts program coordination among community organizations and groups
4. To provide a network of cultural outreach centers for the community
5. To stimulate the consideration of public issues in the light of humanistic values, building such values into the everyday culture of our society
6. To provide the fundamental cultural literacy needed for experience of the arts (484)

Van Fleet and Raber conclude that "the library profession has now accepted the role of providing the opportunities for meaningful use of leisure time, as well as for self-discovery and expression" (494).

"Some debate still exists as to the appropriateness and the function of non-book materials and programming," say Van Fleet and Raber. "Nevertheless, nonprint materials have gained increasing acceptance, and many libraries offer live programming, not simply to encourage use of the library but as a means of sharing the knowledge found there" (494–95).

Programming guru Rhea Joyce Rubin, in *Humanities Programming: A How-to-Do-It Manual* (1997), reported that libraries that offer adult programs cited the following reasons:

- Increase the visibility of the library and community awareness of library resources.
- Provide information and education in a variety of ways to meet differing learning styles as well as diverse educational needs.
- Offer an alternative to commercial entertainment.
- Make the library vital for users of non-books as well as print readers.
- Demonstrate viability to government leaders, taxpayers, and funding agencies.
- Increase circulation.
- Provide a public forum for the exchange of ideas.
- Develop cooperation with other community agencies and organizations.
- Engage diverse participants.
- Expand the library's sphere of influence. (5–6)

"Traditionally the public library has been the source of education and recreation for the out-of-school adult," Rubin says. "The public library was heavily involved in the adult education movements of the 1930s and 1940s. In librarianship, adult education stemmed from reading guidance but differentiated itself by emphasizing group work and formalized programming. Adult education, according to Margaret E. Monroe, had 'an emphasis on purposeful reading, a stress on the library's materials as sources of ideas to be put to use, and a fulfillment of the [library's] commitment to a democratic society.' As a center for adult independent learning, the library supplied resources for self-education and supplemented this education with personalized reading lists and curricula, tutorials, and humanities programs such as book discussions and lecture series" (4–5).

Where Does My Library Fit In?

Making a case for your library's leadership in cultural programming is only the first step in a continuous cycle of determining the appropriate role for your library in planning cultural programming, including setting specific goals and objectives, implementing activities, and evaluating the outcomes to guide planning.

To be effective, programming must be an intentional part of the library's mission. Commitment at all levels of management and administration is essential. Libraries that are the most successful in cultural programming also have the benefit of passionate individuals.

When ALA's 1998 survey asked respondents to rate the centrality of adult cultural programming to their library's mission, the results were split: 47.1 percent said it was central, while 45.3 percent said it was not. When survey participants were asked to rate the level of commitment (no, limited, modest, strong, or absolute) to library cultural programming shown by library staff, library management, the library board, the community, and "yourself," the responses tended to fall in the middle ranges. The respondent ("yourself") was the most likely to report absolute commitment, while one in three respondents perceived strong commitment by both library management and staff (p. 12).

When you have determined how to make the case for cultural programming at your library, you will be ready to move on to the next chapter and the work of setting the most meaningful goals for your community. Those goals may relate to reaching underserved audiences/nonusers, visibility for library services, or other issues you identify. See box 1-2 for an example of how the evaluation of one initiative helped define and make a case for its future.

BOX 1-2

CASE: WRITERS LIVE AT THE LIBRARY

A case example illustrates how evaluating the outcomes of one project helped make the case for future programming. In an evaluation of the American Library Association initiative Writers Live at the Library, evaluation consultant Debra Wilcox Johnson found that participating libraries across the project reported many of the same outcomes. Those libraries, having produced a year's worth of literary programming, planned with community involvement and in partnership with another community entity, consistently identified the following benefits of the experience for all involved, which helped to make the case for future literary programming activity:

- The programming brought current and future writers together.
- The series appealed to and affected a diverse group of readers.
- Writers Live helped the libraries reach new audiences.
- The hosting of nationally known writers resulted in community pride in the project.
- Collaboration is important in the success of adult programs in the library.
- The series exposed participants to new ideas and alternative viewpoints.
- The library learned more about how to conduct literary programming.
- The public library is more firmly established as a cultural center in the community.

Native American
Women Writers
on Community

"*Sister Nations* is a lively, challenging, and
entertaining anthology of contemporary Indian
women's voices. Heid Erdrich and Laura Tohe have
collected prose and poetry that will provoke, amuse,
console, and transform their audiences. *Sister Nations*
is a valuable document and an artistic gift."
—Valerie Miner, author of
The Low Road and *Range of Light*

ikwewag diibaajimowag — *the women are telling stories*

The Friends of the Saint Paul Library, Saint Paul, Minnesota

CHAPTER 2

Planning

*From Goals to Evaluation
and Back Again*

*The difference between where we are
(current status) and where we want to be
(vision and goals) is what we do (target
objectives and action plans).*
      —NATIONAL SCHOOL BOARDS ASSOCIATION

Developing Goals and Objectives

Whether you are already in the midst of making your library the center for community and cultural programming or envisioning what your library could and will be, setting goals and objectives will

- clarify your thinking and communicate your intent;
- provide a map and reference for following through and managing changes;
- enable you and others to evaluate and complete the planning cycle for the future.

Goals are the big picture and tend to remain constant for longer periods, while objectives or strategies tend to be shorter term, more directly measurable activities or outcomes. The goals you identify may relate to your intended audience, your library's collections, themes or issues, or your community. Or they may relate to specific programs. The following sample goals and objectives for cultural programming show the possible range of generality and specificity:

Goal

Reach new immigrant populations in the library service area.

Objective

Collaborate with community members of target populations to develop programming of interest.

Goal

Increase percentage of service population attending programming.

Objectives

Create program offerings to appeal to interests reflected in circulation trends.

Host focus group to determine barriers to program attendance for nonattendees; make appropriate accommodations.

Make visits to meetings of groups outside the library.

Goal

Develop community interest in appreciation of excellent poetry.

Objectives

Expand use of library poetry collection.

Expand size, variety, and quality of library poetry collection.

Host discussions of award-winning poetry facilitated by popular literary figure in community.

Goal

Develop library programming related to year-long library theme of "Immigration and Migration."

Objectives

Engage scholars from local community college to present book and film discussion programs and lecture series bimonthly.

Invite three local immigrant organizations to cohost/sponsor programs.

Goal

Take action to address current issue of economic redlining in community.

Objectives

Provide space for community forum featuring local leaders.

Produce display of materials on topic.

Create website with links to more information and action agendas.

Goal

Seek opportunities for collaboration with League of Women Voters to address upcoming election issues.

Objectives

Link to League website from library site.

Develop bibliography in collaboration with League.

Ask League to provide list of issues and potential speakers and to moderate panel series.

Goal

Fill community void left by closure of local theater center.

Objectives

Provide space for practice or performance by theater troupe members.

Develop programs of interest to theater's audience.

Goal

Seek/establish ways to support library programming over longer term.

Objectives

Host a series of feasibility discussions with opinion makers.

Develop/implement fund-raising plan.

Evaluation of Progress

Once you have determined your goals and the objectives/strategies to reach them, you will need to determine how to measure progress toward those goals. What will success look like? How will you know if you have achieved it? What information will help you determine success, and how will you collect that information? Perhaps some of your goals will not be achieved in the time frame you indicate, but you should be able to measure progress, and you should also be able to use the information you collect for planning, including making your case all over again.

For each goal you set, determine measurable or observable targets and a time frame. You may be required to gather information up front. For example, if you wish to increase circulation of your poetry collection, you will need to quantify current usage for comparison. If you want to increase the participation of a certain population in programming, you will have to find a way to measure or observe current participation and participation at a later time.

Keep in mind that you will want to collect information of two kinds for the purposes of making your case in the future: quantitative and qualitative. Quantitative measures include things you can count, such as number of program attendees (never estimate, always count!) or circulation statistics. Qualitative measures are the stories: the letter from a patron describing how a program changed her life, the comment overheard by a visitor you have never seen in the library before, the presenter who gained a new sense of his work from talking with an audience, or the anonymous donor inspired by the library's activity (yes, this has happened!).

Among the ways to collect information are questionnaires, interviews, numbers gathering, use of existing data, observation, and logs or activity reports.

Questionnaires

If you use questionnaires or evaluation forms, think carefully about what information you want and how you will use it. Among the areas you may want to address are audience characteristics (demographic data), program characteristics (how attendees found out about a program, how much they liked it), and future programs (what community members would like to see). Make your questionnaire easy to answer, be specific in your questions, and make sure that you are not collecting information you already have or are not prepared to act upon if appropriate.

Questionnaires can take many forms and lengths. Figure 2-1 shows a questionnaire developed by the University of Michigan–University of Washington How Libraries Help project and used to evaluate the King County (Wash.) Library System's Voices from the Rim series, held in September 2001 as a way to expose the public to the many cultures of the Pacific Rim. The research objective was to study the attendees' social connectedness and to describe the ways cultural programs provide attendees with opportunities to develop new relationships with people and/or deepen relationships with people they are already connected to.

Interviews

Interviewing may be one-on-one, as in a telephone survey, or group-based, as in a focus group. Questions in an interview are often more open-ended than they are in a written questionnaire, and follow-up questioning can be pursued. Figure 2-2 shows the format of telephone interviews that followed the Voices from the Rim program questionnaire shown in figure 2-1. The interview questions were designed to evaluate the longer-term impact of the programming.

Focus groups are another popular way to get feedback, especially in an invitational setting in which the viewpoints of specific segments of the population are desired.

Numbers Gathering

Numbers provide many kinds of information for evaluation. Some numbers you already collect and need only to be analyzed. Others need to be collected or otherwise sought out. Examples of numbers gathering include

counting attendees at programs and analyzing the numbers over time to look for patterns;

FIGURE 2-1   Sample Program Evaluation Questionnaire

Survey # _____   Staff/Researcher _____ Date _____

Program _____ Location _____

Evaluation Survey

> We are researchers from the University of Washington studying libraries and community programs. Please help us evaluate this program by completing the following questions. Your responses will be confidential. The survey will take just a few minutes.

How long did it take you to get here?   ❑ 0–10 min.   ❑ 10–30 min.   ❑ 30–60 min.   ❑ over 1hour

When did you decide to come?   ❑ today   ❑ yesterday   ❑ last week   ❑ last month

Why did you decide to come to this program?

_____

_____

_____

What did you expect to see/do at this program?

_____

_____

_____

How did you hear about this program?   ❑ friend   ❑ relative   ❑ library   ❑ colleague
(*check all that apply*)   ❑ newspaper   ❑ radio   ❑ Internet   ❑ other _____

Have you been to other programs like this within the past year?   ❑ Yes   ❑ No
If Yes, what kind of programs (dance programs, lectures, etc.)?

_____

_____

Where were the programs held? _____

_____

To what extent as a result of this program, did you? (Please tell us more about this in the space provided).

(*circle one*)

	Not at all				To a great extent
Develop a new skill or learn something new?	1	2	3	4	5
Get motivated to do something?	1	2	3	4	5
Make a connection with someone or something?	1	2	3	4	5
Get pleasure, feel entertained?	1	2	3	4	5

What part of this program did you find the most connection with? Why?

_____

_____

_____

	no connection		(*circle one*)		very strong connection
How strong was the connection?	1	2	3	4	5

What was the most important or helpful part of this program for you? Please explain:

_____

_____

_____

Based on your experience today, what would you tell other people about this program?

_____

_____

_____

How many people came in your group? ❑ 1 (yourself) ❑ 2 ❑ 3 ❑ 4 ❑ 5

Is your group made up of: ❑ family ❑ friends ❑ colleagues ❑ other _____

How often do you see people in your group? ❑ daily ❑ weekly ❑ monthly

Did you talk with anyone at this program that you knew already? ❑ Yes ❑ No
   If Yes, who? ❑ friend ❑ relative ❑ library staff ❑ colleague ❑ other _____

Do you have a King County library card? ❑ Yes ❑ No

Have you ever been to this library before? ❑ Yes ❑ No

How often do you use this library? ❑ First time ❑ Yearly ❑ Every few months ❑ Monthly
   ❑ Weekly ❑ Daily

How many times did you go to *any* library this summer? ❑ 0 ❑ 1–5 ❑ 6–10 ❑ 11+

Gender: ❑ Male ❑ Female
Marital Status: ❑ Single ❑ Married
Have Children: ❑ Yes ❑ No

Age: _____   Occupation: _____

What is your ethnic background? _____

We would like to contact you by phone in about 3 weeks for a brief follow-up interview. If you are willing to participate, please provide the following information so we may contact you:

Name: _____ Phone Number: ( ) _____

Best days/times to call: _____

Thank you!

FIGURE 2-2 Sample Program Follow-Up Telephone Survey Script

Survey # _____ Staff/Researcher _____ Date _____

Program _____ Location _____

Follow-Up Telephone Survey

> I am calling to follow up on a survey you completed at the King County Library. We would like to ask you a few questions about the Voices of the Rim event you attended on _____. Is this a good time? The survey will take only a few minutes.

1. What did you see or do at the _____ event that you remember most?

2. Did you talk about the event with anyone afterwards? If yes:
   a. Who were they?
   b. How often do you see them?
   c. Why did it come up?
   d. Context and format of the discussion?

3. Have you had any contact with anyone that you just met at the event (i.e., had not known before)?
   a. Who were they?
   b. How often do you see them?
   c. Why did it come up?
   d. Context and format of the discussion?

4. Did you bring anything home from the event? If yes:
   a. What was it? (e.g., flyer, crafts, contact info, reference info, etc.)
   b. What did you do with it? (e.g., followed up, put on file, read a book on the subject, etc.)
   c. What else would you plan/like to do with it?

5. Has the event given you any ideas that you would like to follow up on? If yes:
   a. What?
   b. Why is this important to you?

6. What did you see as the most relevant or important that you experienced or gained at the event?

7. Have you done anything new or different because of what you experienced at the

   _____ event?

Thank you!

---

counting circulation in a particular subject range before and after programming;

reviewing overall circulation numbers and overall gate counts over time and in relation to special events and seasons;

counting numbers of presenters and collaborating organizations;

charting funds raised for programming and since the introduction of programming;

measuring column inches of programs' press coverage;

comparing population statistics to cardholder percentage over time.

Use of Existing Data

Existing data useful to evaluation may include census or demographic information, studies or research by other groups (such as an ALA survey of cultural programming for adults in public libraries), or numbers gathered for other or related purposes, such as the reasons outlined above.

Observation

Information that can be gathered by observation includes overheard informal commentary, some general demographics, questions asked or body language at programs, administrative or logistic situations (such as not having enough chairs in the room), and interactions among attendees.

Logs or Activity Reports

A typical activity report might contain a listing of program titles, times, dates, presenters, and attendance. Another might log questions asked of presenters at a particular program. Still another might collect comments or other impact stories about how the programming made a difference to individuals. Specific funders or administrative bodies may require reports of particular information. Regardless of your methods, ultimately, the information you collect will tell you both how you are progressing toward your goals and how you made a difference.

Now you are ready to put your plan into words. Figure 2-3 provides a worksheet for outlining your vision, setting goals and objectives, and measuring outcomes. Be sure to indicate how and when you will measure progress toward your goals.

Planning Calendar

Once you have completed your goal-setting worksheet, you have your basic vision. To start laying out details, use a planning calendar. The planning calendar shown in figure 2-4, for a one-season series of programs, is adapted from *Let's Talk about It: A Planner's Manual* (Moores and Rubin 1984). Use it as a starting point in your planning and adapt it as you go.

FIGURE 2-3 Worksheet for Goal-Setting

Library mission statement
Vision for library's programming and cultural role
GOAL 1
Objectives/strategies
How and when progress will be measured
GOAL 2
Objectives/strategies
How and when progress will be measured
GOAL 3
Objectives/strategies
How and when progress will be measured

FIGURE 2-4 Planning Calendar

Four to Six Months in Advance	Write goals and objectives.
	Discuss series with library board and staff.
	Develop list of potential funding sources.
	Form series planning committee, including:
	    Program director
	    Content adviser(s)/artist(s)/scholar(s)
	    Marketing/graphic arts staff
	    Community member(s) representing target audience
	    Partner representative(s)
	    Friends of the Library
	    Other: _____
	Contact potential funding sources.

Three to Four Months in Advance	Hold first planning committee meeting.
	    Review goals and objectives.
	    Discuss theme and content.
	    Discuss format and presenter possibilities.
	    Develop planning calendar.
	    Discuss fund-raising strategies.
	    Discuss marketing strategies and involvement of others.
	    Determine location.
	    Determine next steps and make assignments for individual members to follow up.
	    Set up e-mail list to keep members updated.
	Research and contact potential funders; write grant proposals, if necessary.
	Contact additional partners and individuals to be involved.
	Research and contact potential presenters; determine their presentation needs.
	Set schedule of programs.
	Reserve program space.
	Finalize budget.

Two Months in Advance	Hold second planning committee meeting.
	    Finalize theme/content, schedule of programs.
	    Finalize publicity/outreach plan.
	Contract with presenters.
	Secure funding.
	Develop marketing and promotional materials.
	Develop/secure programming content materials and equipment.

Six Weeks in Advance	Contact community leaders, library trustees. Implement marketing and promotional strategies. Be sure program materials, books, and other materials/equipment are available (such as films, instruments, special audiovisual equipment). Contact local bookseller or other providers.

(cont.)

FIGURE 2-4   Planning Calendar (*cont.*)

One Month in Advance	Follow up with presenters; seek any additional information or material needed.
	Print and distribute promotion materials.
	Set up displays.
	Begin preregistering participants, if necessary.
One Week in Advance	Give reminder to presenter, planning committee, volunteers.
	Prepare introductions for presenters.
	Make special arrangements for
	child care;
	accessibility;
	contingency plan;
	additional services and clean-up.
	Present details at all-staff meeting; distribute staff fact sheet.
Day of Program	Confirm volunteer availability and assignments.
	Check in with presenter.
	Give reminder to staff.
	Check readiness of program space.
Immediately following Each Program	Jot down attendance count, notes on what worked or didn't work, and things to fine-tune before next program.
After Series	Log progress toward goals.
	Send thank-you notes to presenters.
	Thank planning committee members, staff, others.
	Officially recognize contributors and partners (also during program).
	Write letter to the editor expressing thanks to volunteers and participants and reporting on results.
	Prepare required reports to funders, partners, library administration/board as necessary.
	Meet with committee to assess completed series and begin planning next series.

Program Series Planning Worksheet

When you are ready to get specific about the programs you will present, outline the details on a worksheet such as the one in figure 2-5. Complete all but the last column in advance. Planning and evaluation will include anticipating audience sizes in advance and counting actual attendees at the events. You will also want to spell out plans for publicity, collection development, staffing, and the roles of partners.

FIGURE 2-5   Program Series Planning Worksheet

Title of Series/Theme:

Program/ Event (title/formats)	Sponsors/ Funders to Be Thanked at Program	Presenter (names and/or descriptors)	Location (part of library or specified off-site location)	Planned Date (tentative or scheduled)	Anticipated Attendance (number)	Actual Attendance (actual head count)

Publicity Plan

Collection Development Plan

Staffing/Volunteer Plan

Identification and Roles of Partners/Collaborators

Budgeting

The worksheet provided in figure 2-6 contains basic categories you will want to think about as you set the budget for your program series. The Description column includes typical categories of expenses you may encounter. Under Method of Computation, indicate how you arrived at your figures. For example:

Presenter fees: 3 presenters × $250 each

Collection development: 50 poetry volumes × average $15 each

Because many funding sources look for evidence of matching funds or other cost sharing, you may want to record both actual cash costs and in-kind costs in the Amount column. Thus, if a local printer is donating services valued at $800 to print a postcard mailer promoting your program series, you would enter $800 as an in-kind cost.

Finally, consider a variety of sources for underwriting your program expenses. Sources may differ in the kinds of costs they are willing to subsidize. For example, a local arts agency may fund only artists' fees, whereas the Friends of the Library may be happy to fund refreshments.

FIGURE 2-6 Program Series Budget Worksheet

Description	Method of Computation	Amount (cash or in-kind)	Source
Staff and volunteer time			
Presenter fees			
Presenter travel/ lodging and hospitality			
Promotion expense Design Printing Postage Advertising			
Program materials Design/printing Purchase Distribution			
Collection development			
Facilities Space rental Equipment rental Refreshments			
Other			
Contingency			

CHAPTER 3

Building Participation
Developing Audiences and Interactive Engagement

Culture relates to objects and is a phenomenon of the world; entertainment relates to people and is a phenomenon of life.
—HANNAH ARENDT

The Kansas City Public Library Marketing Department, Kansas City, Missouri

In *A New Framework for Building Participation in the Arts*, a report based on a Rand survey, McCarthy and Jinnett (2001, 2–3) observe that in public policy and in literature about the arts, the focus has changed in recent years from concern with the supply and quality of the arts to increasing public access to and experience with the arts. Libraries, too, have become more aware of and concerned with their audiences and their engagement and no longer focus solely on the quality and depth of collections and administrative concerns.

What Is the Library Audience?

The nation's public libraries attract audiences that are diverse in race, cultural background, ethnicity, age, and educational and economic levels. Unique among cultural and educational institutions and organizations, public libraries have no admission criteria.

Surveys reveal a broad, inclusive library audience. More than six in ten adults (65 percent) use a public library at least once a year. Libraries are used almost equally by men (63 percent) and women (68 percent). And library audiences are racially diverse: a majority of European Americans (65 percent), African Americans (63 percent), Latinos (58 percent), Asian/Pacific Islanders (72 percent), and Native Americans (65 percent) are library users.

In a March 2002 survey conducted by KRC Research and Consulting, respondents indicated that they most often use the library for educational purposes (46 percent), followed by entertainment (41 percent), and 90 percent of the total respondents believed that libraries are places of opportunity for education and self-help and offer free access for all. Of those who had used a public library in person in the previous year, 14 percent heard a speaker, saw a movie, or attended a special program.

In comparison, a 1997 survey by the National Endowment for the Arts found that 50 percent of adults had attended a performance in one of seven performing arts (jazz, classical music, opera, musicals, nonmusical plays, ballet, or other dance) or had visited an art museum in the previous year (1998, 14). This group is smaller than the group that uses libraries, but its members attend programs in larger numbers.

For most academic libraries, the audience is a community made up of students and faculty, others affiliated with the institution, and individuals who live and work in the larger community in which the institution is based. School libraries operate in a similar community of students, faculty, staff, parents, and, to a varying degree, the surrounding community, while the audiences for special libraries tend to be limited to the host organization's staff and clientele. Like the other clientele of library types, the audiences for special libraries may have a variety of demographic characteristics, abilities, and interests in the organization.

Although library audiences are vast (almost every American has access to a library of some kind) and are served democratically for the most part, it is important to recognize that a library cannot be all things to all people and that it must develop and package its offerings in ways that reach targeted segments of its audience.

Why Target Your Audience?

Many librarians, when asked to describe their target audience for a particular program or series, answer with some variation of "the general public," or "library users," or "the people who come through the doors." Though such an approach is inclusive, it is not likely to result in the best or largest audience.

Given the diversity of populations that libraries serve and the range of educational and entertainment options, it is important to identify and target specific audiences. Identifying the audience you want to reach as part of your goal-setting and planning process will help you to identify the most effective presenters, include members of that audience in your planning and publicity, and collaborate with appropriate organizations, and will result in an engaged and appreciative audience.

According to the Rand survey analyzed in *A New Framework* (McCarthy and Jinnett 2001, 21), organizations tend to identify and target audiences solely by sociodemographic indicators about their backgrounds, but motivations and attitudes are the attributes that actually contribute to an individual's decision to participate, and those can be influenced. Moreover, individual participation decisions are complex and recurring—based on demographic, personality, cultural, and practical factors as well as on prior experiences with and attitudes toward arts participation. Libraries need to be able to effectively gather information on such factors in order to influence participation.

As reported in the 2001 Rand survey, organizations perceived that people were motivated to participate in the arts for specific reasons. Those reasons parallel the reasons people take part in library cultural programming. They include

- Personal interest in the material itself (over 90 percent)
- Opportunity for social interaction (about 70 percent)
- Interest in learning about the arts (over 60 percent)
- Accompanying a friend or family member (about 55 percent)
- Education and enrichment (about 55 percent)
- Publicity surrounding the event (about 30 percent)
- Desire to express themselves artistically (about 25 percent)
- Community responsibility (over 20 percent)
- Civic responsibility (about 8 percent) (p. 86)

Experiences in library programming bear out the Rand finding that personal interest in the material itself, whether or not associated with demographic indicators, is the strongest motivator. For example, when Flint, Michigan, served as a pilot site in the American Library Association's Writers Live at the Library program, the library's planning committee worked with a number of organizations to plan and cosponsor individual programs, focusing on artists who reflected both the interests and the characteristics of cosponsoring groups. Working with a local African American book club, the library scheduled a visit by the renowned literary and mystery novelist Walter Mosley, and with the local Vietnam Veterans of America chapter, they invited Larry Heinemann, the author of the Pulitzer Prize–winning *Paco's Story*. The Genesee Valley Indian Center cosponsored the appearance of James Welch, a critically acclaimed Native American author.

Another library in the Writers Live pilot project invited author Stuart Dybek for a series of programs in which Dybek pegged the content of his poetry and fiction to the audience for each event. At a Rotary luncheon attended by a predominantly male audience, he read from a nostalgic and humorous story about the foibles of an eccentric father from the perspective of his teenage son. In a junior high school class, he talked about writing as a career and led a group writing exercise. At a library program for a writers' group, he read from poetry and short stories with more complex adult themes and answered questions about writing.

Reaching the Underserved

The underserved population can be defined in many ways. Perhaps you seek a more diverse audience, or a larger audience, or a more meaningful or challenging experience for a current audience. To be effective in programming that reaches diverse, underserved, or any targeted audiences, consider the most important elements in building participation:

Determine who the programming is for. Audiences may be identified not only by demographic (such as age, ethnicity, education, and income) but also by geographic and behavioral indicators. Programming for older, low-income adults with transportation issues who appreciate folk music will differ from programming for an audience made up of college-bound Latino teenagers interested in socializing with peers while pursuing arts activities related to academic interests and requirements.

Invite voices to the table. Work with groups and individuals to identify and attract desired audiences. Collaborating with organizations and presenters serving and drawn from the target audience can provide insights into the motivations and attitudes held by that group. Such working partners can also influence and deliver their membership, affiliates, fans, and other clientele.

Identify and remove barriers to participation. Motivations, perceptions, and practical concerns all present potential barriers to participation for individuals. Among the practical and personal barriers are child-care problems, inaccessibility, unfamiliarity, inconvenient hours or location, lack of time or peers to come with, interference of other activities, and lack of understanding. Perceptual barriers include lack of appeal, discomfort, and elitism.

Allow others to share ownership. Your collaborating organizations, the library staff and board, funding agencies, media, and local politicians and businesses—all should be made to feel welcome. True collaboration means that many groups and individuals participate in planning and therefore have a stake in the outcomes.

Answering questions and gathering information that will address participation in the planning process can take many forms, from informal discussions with staff, community, planning committee members, potential presenters and performers, and collaborating organizations, to formal surveys, marketing studies, and focus groups.

Counting Up: What Is the Optimum Audience Size?

Reaching the right audience might be one goal; getting a large audience is another. Anyone who has ever put on a program has fretted and sweated about (and provided justification for) audience size. Attendance figures are one way in which libraries measure success. However, not every program is designed or meant to draw a standing-room-only audience.

In the 1998 ALA survey, the total attendance for all programs for adults offered annually by libraries ranged widely, with the highest one-year attendance total reported to be over 10,000 (7.0 percent; ALA/PPO 1999a). Nearly half the libraries reported annual attendance of 500 or less (48.4 percent; iv). In addition to variation in numbers of programs, libraries reported significant variance among program types, which seemed to reflect the nature of the programming as well as regional and other differences. The intensity of participation (or the individual effort required to participate) may be a factor in the program types with the smallest groups. For example, book discussion and creative writing workshops, which typically require an intense level of preparation, were typically attended by fewer than twenty people in most of the libraries.

The intensity of participation units (IPU) formula developed by Frannie Ashburn, director of the North Carolina Center for the Book, as a handout for workshops on cultural programming, illustrates that the intensity of the participant experience is generally in inverse proportion to the number of participants, so that simple audience counts might not tell the whole story of the value of the investment in programming. For example, a large auditorium-style event with a well-known speaker may draw a crowd of two hundred or many more, and a traveling exhibition may be seen by thousands, while a five-part book discussion or a four-part writing workshop may be attended by twenty-five persons per session. The difference is in (1) the amount of time the participant must invest in preparing for, attending, and participating in the activity and (2) the relative amount of lasting cognitive growth derived from active participation in the activity.

For those who really want to get a big number, Ashburn suggests the IPU formula to illustrate the impact of events with the following four examples:

One-hour lecture with question-and-answer session attended by 200 people:

200 people × 1 hour = <u>200 IPUs</u>

*One Let's Talk about It discussion series
attended by 25 people:*

25 people × 40 hours* = <u>1,000 IPUs</u>

* 40 hours = 10 hours of attendance at programs at the library
(5 programs @ 2 hours each) + 30 hours of reading (5 books
@ 6 hours—a low estimate—preparing for the programs)

*One documentary film viewing/discussion series
attended by 25 people:*

25 people × 15 hours[†] = <u>375 IPUs</u>

[†] 15 hours = 12 hours of attendance at programs (6 programs
@ 2 hours each) + 3 hours of reading (6 programs @ ½ hour
of reading in preparation for each program)

*One poetry reading/viewing/listening/discussion series
attended by 25 people:*

25 people × 18 hours[‡] = <u>450 IPUs</u>

[‡] 18 hours = 12 hours of attendance at programs at the library
(6 programs @ 2 hours each) + 6 hours of reading (6 programs
@ 1 hour of reading in preparation for each program)

According to Ashburn, "Even though the one-hour lecture draws a crowd eight times larger than any one program in a series, the participation quotient is higher for a series. And people do get more out of things they actively participate in—reading, viewing, discussing. In other words, your value received is commensurate with your input."

Finally, determining the right number of participants for any event or series should be a function of initial planning in conjunction with the type of programming and demographic of the target audience. It is important to estimate the expected audience size accurately and to avoid predicting an unrealistically large number for every event. Anticipate and count actual attendees to help in analyzing activities and planning for future programs.

Once you have defined and targeted your audiences and thought about what motivates them, it is time to look for appropriate collaborators to help you reach them.

CHAPTER 4

Collaboration

Collaboration doesn't necessarily make the work easier, but it makes the programming better. —DEBRA WILCOX JOHNSON

Collaboration really does make programming better. Fresh ideas, more meaningful programming, great resources, larger and different audiences, and relationships that will enrich future endeavors are just some of the payoffs of the hard work of successful collaboration.

Who Collaborates? Friends and Other Partners

Library Friends groups are key collaborators for adult programming. Three out of four public libraries collaborate with the Friends of the Library (74 percent), and funding is the most common contribution from the Friends group to adult programming (91 percent), according to the ALA 1998 survey (ALA/PPO 1999a, 10–11). Other important contributions by Friends include refreshments, audience, volunteers, and publicity. Half of public libraries also work with Friends groups when planning cultural programs.

Most libraries collaborate with at least one outside group when offering cultural programming. The most frequently reported collaborators were arts groups (40 percent), historical societies (33 percent), community-based organizations (32 percent), newspapers (30 percent), and writers' groups (24 percent). Others reported, in descending order, were local business, bookstores, museums, service clubs, primary and secondary schools, other libraries, four-year colleges and universities, literacy programs, radio stations, drama groups, television stations, and two-year/community colleges.

The ways in which libraries collaborate with outside groups are varied. The principal contributions made by such groups have been program presenters (57 percent), publicity (54 percent), and audience/program attendees (45 percent). Other ways outside groups contribute include becoming involved in planning/advice, supplying funds, providing volunteers for program tasks, and furnishing refreshments for programs. A few also provide facilities or space for the program, equipment, printing services, or other assistance.

For any type of library, collaboration is a sure-fire way to develop audiences. When you collaborate with other groups to develop and present programs, they can bring along their own member audiences and add richness and relevance to content. Partners can provide both program and presenter ideas, and help the library tap into new audiences. Among the effective partnerships from past applicants to the ALA's LIVE! @ your library initiative were local schools and colleges (especially community colleges), arts and writers' organizations, and community groups whose members were target audiences (for example, young adults, ethnic and cultural groups, and issue-based groups).

McCarthy and Jinnett identify similar findings in their report on the Rand study (2001, 75). Arts organizations that collaborated with community groups reported a number of reasons for doing so: to build relations with the community, to promote activities, to share mailing lists, to structure events, to share performance space, to provide legitimacy, to show political support, to gain access to artists, to furnish technical assistance, to advise on programming, and to share resources, such as funds, staff, equipment, and office space.

One Book Events Include Many Partners

One Community, One Book initiatives have become extremely popular and are a very effective way to develop collaborative relationships throughout the community. Maggie Nelson at the Peoria (Ill.) Public Library engaged a broad cast of community partners and supporters when the library launched Peoria Reads! All Peorians were encouraged to read Ernest J. Gaines's *A Lesson before Dying* for this multifaceted One Book, One Community citywide reading program. Community partners listed on the project's events brochure, shown in figure 4-1, ranged from the Peoria Empowerment Committee to the African American Museum and tapped into almost every possible audience in Peoria.

One Bay, One Book, featuring Tom Wolfe's *The Right Stuff*, was organized by the New Port Richey (Fla.) Public Library in October/November 2003 with a large coalition of partners, including Fantasy of Flight aircraft collection, Flightshops at St. Petersburg–Clearwater International Airport, Florida Humanities Council, Hernando County Public Library Systems, Pasco County Library System, Pinellas Public Library Cooperative, St. Petersburg Museum of History, St. Petersburg Times Festival of Reading, Starbucks, and the Tampa Bay Library Consortium. Programs included library and school book discussion groups, film screenings, a trivia contest, and a program at the St. Petersburg Times Festival of Reading.

Lincoln City (Neb.) Libraries partnered with the *Lincoln Journal Star* for One Book, One Lincoln, which featured Ann Patchett's novel *Bel Canto* in the fall of 2003. Additional supporters were KFOR 1240, Lamar Outdoor Advertising, and the Nebraska Humanities Council. The library organized training sessions for interested discussion leaders along with a number of programs at various public libraries during September, October, and November around the themes of *Bel Canto*. The programs included such topics as opera appreciation (presented by the Friends of Opera at the University of Nebraska–Lincoln), language translation, the music of South America, writing techniques, and the different forms love may take.

The Rosenberg Library in Galveston, Texas, presented Galveston Reads: *Tortilla Curtain* (by T. Coraghessan Boyle) in 2003. The book-selection committee recommended three books for consideration to the Galveston Reads committee that included representatives from the *Galveston County Daily News*, University of Texas Medical Branch at Galveston, Texas A&M, Galveston College, Galveston Independent School District, Midsummer Books, Rosenberg Library, and independent citizens. The Galveston Reads committee selected *Tortilla Curtain* as a tribute to Henry Rosenberg, benefactor of the Rosenberg Library, which celebrated its hundredth anniversary in 2004.

ALA Traveling Exhibitions—Case Studies in Collaboration

Libraries hosting traveling exhibitions managed by the American Library Association Public Programs Office have shown a strong ability to leverage local collaboration that adds to the richness of programming on exhibition themes and draws participation from all corners of the community.

FIGURE 4-1 Peoria Reads! Event Brochure Listing Partners

"Peoria Reads!"

Initiated locally by the Peoria Public Library and Common Place, this exciting program is modeled after "One City, One Book" projects in Seattle, Washington; Rochester, New York; Syracuse, New York and Chicago, Illinois.

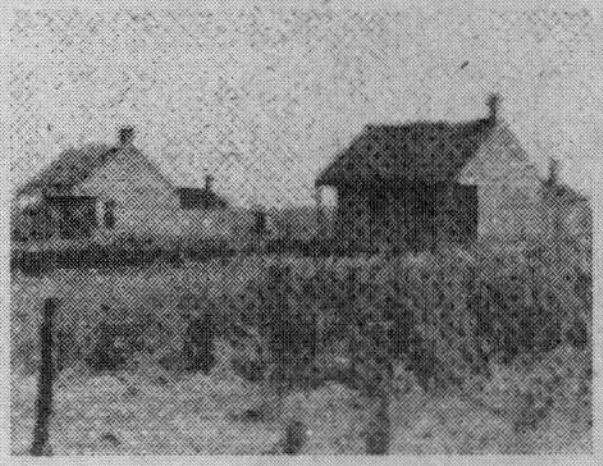

The Goals of "Peoria Reads"

- To bring our community together in ways to promote better understanding of our diverse population.
- To increase opportunities for dialogue among individuals of all ages and backgrounds.
- To broaden and deepen readers' appreciation for books dealing with significant issues.
- To bring more people into libraries, bookstores, and literacy institutions.

Community Partners

Adams Outdoor Advertising
African American Museum
Alliance Library System
American Library Association "Writers Live" Project
Area Colleges and Universities
Barnes & Noble
CityLink
City of Peoria
Common Place
Friends of Peoria Public Library
Illinois Central College
Lincoln Middle School Builder's Club
National City Bank
Peoria Area Community Foundation
Peoria Empowerment Committee
Peoria Federation of Teachers
Peoria Journal Star
Peoria Housing Authority
Peoria Public Library
Peoria School District
Regional Office of Education
Robert Morris College
Tri-County Urban League
WTVP Channel 47

Partners list March 13, 2002

March and April 2002

Peoria Reads!

A Lesson Before Dying

by Ernest J. Gaines

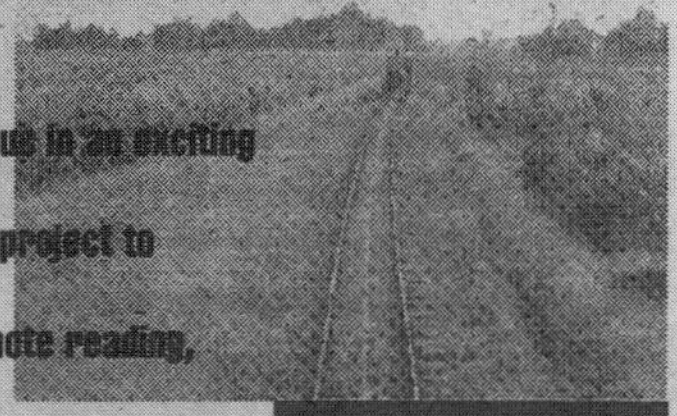

Join us in an exciting new project to promote reading, spark discussion, and bring our community together because of one significant book. Then take part in a variety of special events scheduled throughout our community.

For more information, call:
CommonPlace
674-3316
or
Peoria Public Library
497-2200

Courtesy of the Peoria Public Library, Peoria, Illinois

Go Figure! *and Outreach to Underserved Groups*

Through children's literature, the ALA traveling exhibition *Go Figure!* in cooperation with the Minnesota Children's Museum brought the exciting world of math and its everyday uses to children two to seven years old and their parents, with representations from many children's books, including *Arthur's Pet Business*, by Marc Brown; *The Doorbell Rang*, by Pat Hutchins; *The Quilt*, by Ann Jonas; *Frog and Toad Are Friends: A Lost Button*, by Arnold Lobel; and *Goldilocks and the Three Bears*, illustrated by James Marshall.

Libraries hosting this exhibition collaborated with local museums, especially Science Discovery museums, to develop programs related to math for children. Other collaborators included service organizations, college education classes, bookstores, and educational groups.

Outreach to underserved parts of the community was required of the libraries on the exhibition tour. Spanish-language exhibit brochures were widely distributed to Spanish-speaking communities. Most libraries worked with local Head Start organizations, the YMCA child-care program, housing projects, literacy coalitions, refugee resource networks, homeless shelters, county health departments, and other social organizations that target at-risk and underserved populations. Many libraries found funding within the community to provide transportation to the library for children from such groups if it was not already available.

Contacts the exhibit fostered between libraries and social services groups will be important in helping libraries create future programs for the parents and children those groups serve. Libraries identified several areas in which the exhibit will influence future outreach for children's programming: (1) they will continue collaborating with community partners such as Head Start, daycare providers, social agencies, and schools on programs for two- to seven-year-olds; (2) they will plan and develop programs that repeatedly expose young special-needs children to books and math concepts at in-house story hours and off-site library programs; (3) they will increase marketing services and resources to better reach local minority and at-risk population groups.

Frankenstein in Ithaca

The community-wide impact of the ALA-sponsored *Frankenstein: Penetrating the Secrets of Nature* traveling exhibition and related programs presented by Tompkins County Public Library in Ithaca, New York, was very strong, thanks to extensive collaboration. Efforts included an open forum at the library attended by more than seventy representatives from the city, local businesses, educational, religious, and other community organizations, a community reading project focused on Mary Shelley's novel *Frankenstein*, bookmarks, newsletters, flyers, and media announcements. The public library worked with Cornell University and other local institutions, organizations, and schools to make the county population of one hundred thousand aware of Frankenstein Festival programs at the library, the university, and other community venues. National Public Radio's *Weekend Edition Sunday* selected the project for a seven-minute feature on its October 29, 2002, program. Local radio stations featured the festival, and the local cable channel did a live broadcast of a community discussion panel on artificial intelligence. During one weekend, all community ministers included Frankenstein themes in their sermons and homilies. Both the library and Cornell University had extensive websites devoted to Frankenstein discussion questions and program information. The collaboration can be credited for an estimated exhibition attendance of fifteen thousand and nearly five hundred participants at seventeen programs. In addition, nearly two thousand high-school students and three thousand incoming freshmen and three hundred faculty members at Cornell University read Mary Shelley's novel as part of their coursework.

Cornell University donated eighteen hundred copies of Mary Shelley's *Frankenstein* to the library. The library used two hundred copies and donated the rest to three community reading centers, the collections of four rural libraries, and to retirement communities, schools, community centers, civic groups, and religious congregations. Borders donated 15 percent of its sales of the book to the library. The book was also available as an e-book on the library website. Used-book stores reported excellent sales of the book. Two reading and discussion groups met at the library, and more than twenty other reading groups met throughout the county to discuss the book.

Cornell University sponsored public programs in addition to course presentations: a Frankenbird contest for pupils up to eighth grade, an extensive film series for the community, monster talks by faculty members, and a video lecture series on the book, available on the Cornell website. The library's seven partners in the local Discovery Trail also presented programs. They included the Cayuga Nature Center, Cornell Lab of Ornithology, Herbert F. Johnson Museum of Art, Tompkins County Museum, the Sciencenter, Cornell Plantations, and the Paleontological Research Institution.

Frankenstein and Collaboration among Libraries

A unique feature of the traveling Frankenstein exhibition is the resulting collaboration of different types of libraries in a community. The tour includes eighty-two libraries in thirty-seven states, a mix of forty-seven public libraries, eight medical libraries, and twenty-seven academic libraries. In a number of locations, public libraries and academic and medical institutions in the same region are working together on programming. Among the benefits of the collaborations are mutual marketing support, stimulating new programming ideas, and useful future contacts.

Given the themes in *Frankenstein* that address personal and societal responsibilities in relation to science and medicine, Cuyahoga County (Ohio) Public Library's Parma regional branch worked with several medical organizations for the first time in creating programs. Parma Community General Hospital, a major local sponsor, awarded the library a grant to underwrite programming, hosted a panel on bioethics, and helped publicize other library programs. The partnership led to more cooperation and more health-related programs for the public. The Bioethics Network of Ohio helped draw an audience to Parma's bioethics panel. As a result of the collaboration, the library and the network are discussing plans for continued programming at Cuyahoga County library branches about ethical issues in research and medicine.

At the University of Arizona at Tucson, the Arizona Health Sciences Library developed a community- and university-wide approach to Frankenstein programming, attracting a large public audience by working with the health sciences center's public affairs office and by naming a diverse group of people to its steering committee. Steering committee members included staff from the Tucson–Pima County (Ariz.) Public Library, which created a promotional display of Frankenstein materials at the main library to introduce patrons to the evening community lecture series and Franken FilmFest at the health center. An attention-grabbing Bride of Frankenstein perched on a medical gurney was the highlight of the display. The Arizona Health Sciences Library offered thirteen Frankenstein programs and presented a Doctor of Frankensteinology diploma to anyone who attended at least five of them.

Working with Community Organizations

According to the authors of the Rand survey analysis, respondents learned several important lessons in the process of building good partnerships:

- Choose an organization with a complementary mission.
- Choose organizations with complementary assets and strengths.
- Build trust: relationships must be perceived as mutually beneficial.
- Understand mutual capabilities.
- Maintain commitment over the long term. (McCarthy and Jinnette 2001, 102–3)

The tips below, which expand on forming community partnerships and working with partners to develop library programs, are adapted from a workshop handout developed by Natalie Cole at the California Center for the Book.

Choosing Collaborating Organizations

Review program goals and objectives (see chapter 2). Which organizational strengths will help you achieve your goals, and which weaknesses might stand in your way? How could potential program partners build on your strengths and compensate for your weaknesses? If you are trying to bring underserved constituents into the library, consider partnering with an organization that serves the constituents you are trying to attract. If you have trouble publicizing your programs, you might choose to partner with a media organization, such as a local newspaper, radio, or television station, to help create awareness.

Think about what you want from a program partner. Do you want your partner to be actively involved in organizing the program and guiding its direction? Or do you want to design and create the program and call on your partner to help with marketing, publicizing, and creating awareness?

Think about the benefits you can provide for your program partner. A successful working relationship will benefit both parties, and any potential partner will want to know how it will benefit from the time and resources it gives to the program. For example, will the organization's constituents benefit from participating in the program or becoming more aware of the library? Will the organization receive valuable publicity by partnering with you? How will an ongoing relationship with the library benefit your potential partner?

Research potential partner organizations. Make sure you have up-to-date information about the organizations you plan to contact. Know who they are, what they do, who they serve, and what their achievements are. Talk to other people who have previously worked with the organizations. Find out if you have a friend or colleague in common with the person you plan to contact so that you do not have to cold-call. If you can get a recommendation, or an in, making the contact will be much easier.

Make preliminary contact. During the first communication, let your potential partner know quickly and concisely who you are, why you are calling or e-mailing, and what your proposal is. Find out if you are talking to the right person—the person who can help you most. Be prepared to answer questions and to follow up if the person asks something that you cannot immediately answer. Once you have established who the best person to talk to is, arrange to meet and have a more in-depth conversation at a mutually convenient time.

Meet with a representative of the partnering organization. Before you meet, send background information about the library program, for example, a program plan, a summary or fact sheet, and your business card. At the meeting, discuss your program goals and objectives, your reasons for choosing the organization as your potential partner, and the mutually beneficial results you anticipate coming from the partnership.

Working with a Partner

Establish the terms of the partnership. Clarify the expectations that you have of each other and of the program. Once you have agreed on terms and expectations, do your best to keep them. If you find that you cannot meet some of the expectations outlined at the beginning of the partnership, talk to your partner about them as soon as possible.

Communicate effectively with your partner. Create and maintain a positive working relationship by regularly talking to your partner and listening to what he or she has to say. Show appreciation for your partner's effort. Create opportunities for the two of you to identify and work through problems, challenges, or dissatisfactions.

Communicate effectively with the members of your own organization. Ensure that your staff feel comfortable about working with representatives of the partnering organization. Talk to them about the partnership and discuss with them any apprehensions and concerns they might have. Involve them in the process of choosing program partners.

Once the program is over, follow up. Publicly acknowledge and thank your partner for working to make your program a success. Put your partner on your mailing list and ensure that he or she receives regular updates about library activities. Keep up-to-date with what your partner is doing. If the program was a great success for both of you, start planning another program together!

Planning Committees

In addition to working with organizations, many libraries form planning committees of individuals who are stakeholders and advisers to formulate plans and assist in reaching out as needed. Members of a planning committee may include staff (project director, public relations person, graphics, reader's advisory, and so forth), board members, Friends, representatives of partner organizations, funders, interested community members, specialists in content areas, artists, and others. The group should not be particularly large (five to eight people), and each member should be willing to see the series through from start to finish.

If you want or need input from a larger group, consider a community meeting—a group of thirty to fifty participants who can provide a more general, one-time set of ideas and expectations to a smaller steering committee. The larger group can serve as a core of volunteers and a network for getting the word out. Look for people who will work well together, help you stay focused (and creative), and be enthusiastic about the programming. Identify people you can count on to help you and who have good contacts with the media, presenters, and your target audience(s).

women's history month | march 2002

LIVE!
@ your library™

celebrating
the courage of
women

1877 quasquicentennial 2002
125 years

omaha public library
Everything you want to know. And more.
www.omaha.lib.ne.us

Cover photo: Margaret Sanger (1883 - 1966), nurse and advocate for women and the poor.

celebrating the courage of women
women's history month **LIVE!** @ your library™ march 2002

NEBRASKA WRITER JONIS AGEE
Tuesday March 26 | 6:30 - 7:30 pm
Benson Branch | 60th & Binney | 444-4846
Back by popular demand. Jonis Agee is credited with a long list of awards, popular novels and short story collections. Three of her works, *Strange Angels, Bend This Heart,* and *Sweet Eyes,* were named *Notable Books of the Year* by the *New York Times.*

OMAHA WOMEN ARTISTS EXHIBIT & RECEPTION
Thursday March 7 | 7 pm
Phipps Gallery | 15th & Farnam | 444-4800
Celebrate Women! Works by Omaha artists Mary Zellany, Linda Garcia and women from The Program for Women and Successful Aging will be on display through March 31. Grab a friend and come to the opening reception where you'll enjoy art, live music by Beth McBride, readings and refreshments in the new Phipps Gallery on the main floor of the W. Dale Clark library.

COPING WITH INFERTILITY
Thursday March 14 | 6:30 pm
Phipps Gallery | 15th & Farnam | 444-4800
Dr. C. Maud Doherty and *Today's Omaha Woman* magazine editor Melanie Morrissey Clark (pictured) are co-authors of their new book *The Fertility Handbook: A Guide to Getting Pregnant.* This program will offer insight into the problems of infertility while looking at the alternatives available to families that want children, but are having difficulty.

DEVELOPING FINANCIAL INDEPENDENCE
Tuesday March 12 | 7 pm | W. Dale Clark | 15th & Farnam
Tuesday March 19 | 7 pm | Abrahams Branch | 5111 N. 90th
You'll get concrete, practical advice on how to develop financial goals from one of Omaha's top financial experts. "Life works better when you have goals," says featured presenter Carolin Whitaker, a registered investment advisor who is also a recipient of two national awards for her work with people just like you.

THE BEAUTY MYTH: WOMEN, WEIGHT & APPEARANCES
Saturday March 23 | 3 - 4:30 pm
Abrahams Branch | 5111 N. 90th | 444-6284
Despite the gains of the women's movement, women are still judged by what they look like—and men, by what they do. How can women free themselves from the beauty myth? This presentation focuses on how energy and money are spent on molding women and the ways women are socialized to obsess over their weight and aging. Presented by author of *Fat: A Fate Worse Than Death?*, teacher and women's advocate Ruth Raymond Thone.

MYTHS OF WOMEN'S MADNESS ON THE PLAINS
Monday March 25 | 6:30 - 7:45 pm
Sorensen Branch | 48th & Cass | 444-5274
Focusing on Nebraska women of the late 1800s, this presentation examines the myths -- as they are promoted through fiction and history -- and the realities, based on diaries and journals. The lives of Plains women were as varied and vivid as the pieces of a colorful quilt. Presented by scholar of Great Plains and women's studies Nancy B. Johnson.

omaha public library
Everything you want to know. And more.
www.omaha.lib.ne.us

omaha public library
f OUNDATION
a quasquicentennial celebration sponsor

NEBRASKA HUMANITIES COUNCIL

Courtesy of the Omaha Public Library

CHAPTER 5

Series, Formats, Themes, and Tie-ins
Putting the Pieces Together

Readers transform a library from a mausoleum into many theaters.
—MASON COOLEY

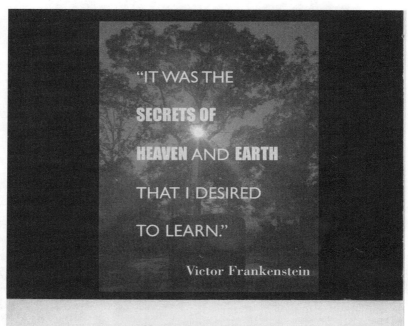

"IT WAS THE SECRETS OF HEAVEN AND EARTH THAT I DESIRED TO LEARN."

Victor Frankenstein

You are cordially invited
to attend the opening reception of
Frankenstein: Penetrating the Secrets of Nature.

Featured Speaker: Robyn L. Schiffman, Department of
Comparative Literature, University of Chicago,
"Frankenstein and the Landscape of Letters"

Where: Moraine Valley Community College
Library, Building L, Second Floor
10900 South 88th Avenue, Palos Hills, Illinois

When: Tuesday, March 30, 2004
6:30 p.m. (program will begin at 7 p.m.)

Light refreshments will be served.

Please RSVP to Mary McCarthy, Moraine Valley Library
(708) 974-5709 by **March 17**.

Courtesy of Moraine Valley Community Library, Palos Hills, Illinois

Most libraries find that series of programs—either a variety of program types or formats and/or programs linked to themes—engage the widest audiences because they offer a range of participation options for attendees. Formats, themes, and tie-in opportunities will vary according to your programming goals but are useful in unifying groups of programs and for expanding visibility.

About Series

Series create a sense of ongoing effort. They provide more opportunity for library and programming visibility, for potential audience participation, and for building momentum, enthusiasm, and identity for the library and its programs. Programmers commonly formulate series by a theme or by recurring format. For example, the Johnson County Central Resource Library in Overland Park, Kansas, used a recurring format in its Writers Place Poetry Reading series, which featured locally and nationally known poets presenting their work on the third Tuesday of every month at 7:00 p.m. Libraries that hosted the American Library Association's traveling exhibition *The Many Realms of King Arthur* used the exhibition's themes to develop series of programs during their six-week exhibition period. The Peter White Library's programming in Marquette, Michigan, was typical of efforts throughout the country. According to its final report on its participation, the library presented an extensive lecture series, with weekly presentations by local scholars on such topics as women in the Middle Ages, the search for the Holy Grail, life in a medieval castle, Arthurian magic and mysticism in the New Age, cathedral building, Arthurian film, and courtly love and chivalry. The opening reception was well publicized in local media, lectures were well attended, a castle-building contest created attention, the book discussion series was comprehensive, and a medieval fair drew more than a thousand people.

Program Formats

Format refers to the way participants will experience a program. Will it be a lecture or panel discussion? A facilitated discussion of a book? A film or exhibition? A musical performance? A combination? In this chapter, program formats are discussed under five general categories: presentations, participatory discussions, performances, exhibitions, and book festivals.

Presentations

Presentations include events in which artists, scholars, or other experts present and comment upon their own work or the work or ideas of others. Presentations may be introduced or moderated in a variety of ways and may include direct or indirect audience participation.

AUTHOR AND LITERARY PRESENTATIONS

Author and literary presentations take a number of forms and often encompass a number of activities. Among the most common formats for author readings and presentations are

- an author reading from a published work or work in progress, with an audience question-and-answer session followed by a book signing;
- an author talk on writing, publishing, or genres;
- a panel discussion by a number of authors;
- a poetry reading, slam, or commemorative reading;
- an author-led discussion with an audience of writers or aspiring writers.

Writers may be asked to read from their own published works and in-progress works and to talk on topics ranging from creativity to the way a book evolves during the writing process to the pitfalls of autobiography. They can participate in panel dialogues with other writers, information discussions with older or younger audiences, and writing workshops for local writers. Some writers perform readings with musical accompaniment. In addition, libraries have found that pairing better-known with lesser-known writers for a reading can be an effective way to build interest and expand audiences for both.

Author presentations often take forms that are more than readings. In Monroe, Michigan, as part of the Writers Live at the Library series, the writer Al Young performed a reading of his poetry with musical accompaniment by the high-school jazz band. The public library cosponsored the event with a local theater, where the event was presented. A reception for press, library supporters, and community dignitaries preceded the performance, and a book sale and autographing session followed. While visiting Monroe, Young also read his work and talked about his writing at a residential home for teenage boys.

In Chicago, at the Harold Washington Library Center, the MacArthur-award-winning author Colson Whitehead read aloud from published works and work in progress and then was interviewed by his friend, the acclaimed poet, critic, and university professor Kevin Young. The reading, combined with the interview, shed additional light on the work of both authors.

At the Peoria (Ill.) Public Library, poets Kevin Stein (later named Illinois poet laureate) and Cinda Thompson shared their experiences growing up in the Midwest in the program "Family Stories: Poems and Conversations."

Critic, poet, and biographer Diane Middlebrook, author of books on Anne Sexton, Billy Tipton, and Sylvia Plath and Ted Hughes, has made presentations featuring readings of her work, discussion of the art and science of the biographer, and even brief dramatizations at libraries. At Stanford, where Middlebrook is a professor of English emerita and Tobias Wolff is a faculty member, the university featured Wolff's book *In Pharaoh's Army: Memories of the Lost War* as the 2003 One Book selection and launched the initiative on campus with a conversation between Middlebrook and Wolff during Reunion Homecoming Weekend in October.

CREATIVE WRITING WORKSHOPS

Often held in conjunction with readings and panels for a literary festival or residency by a single author or English professor, writing workshops are generally offered to smaller groups of people and may be organized as a series.

LECTURES

Lecture formats are fitting for authors, historians, artists, scientists, literary scholars, critics, essayists, columnists, and others. Most lecturers will speak on a specific topic and may use slides, PowerPoint presentations, film, or audio clips.

Villanova University's Falvey Memorial Library hosts a distinguished lecture series twice each academic year. The goal is "to emphasize the link between libraries, and creative and intellectual endeavors." Speakers have included Dr. Ruth Kluger reading from her memoir *Still Alive: A Holocaust Girlhood Remembered* and John F. Andrews, founder and president of the Shakespeare Guild, lecturing on "A Shakespearean Tragedy: The Booth Family of Actors and the Assassination of Abraham Lincoln." In university environments, such programs are usually cosponsored with relevant academic departments, clubs, and community groups.

The Rosamund Gifford Lecture Series, a fund-raiser sponsored by the Friends of the Central Library, Onondaga County Public Library, in Syracuse, New York, is described by the library as "the largest library-related lecture series in the United States." The 2003 to 2004 lineup lived up to the library's billing as "world-class authors with a variety of viewpoints" talking about "their craft, their lives, and what's on their minds." The six lecturers, featured once a month in October though December and March through May, were journalist Anna Quindlen, young-adult novelist Laurie Halse Anderson, interior design author Chris Casson Madden, first novelist Julie Glass, U.S. Poet Laureate Billy Collins, and novelist Michael Chabon.

Conversations with Artists, Portsmouth Public Library's artist lecture series in New Hampshire provides regional artists—painters, sculptors, musicians, and writers—opportunities to present their work, discuss their craft and motivation, and answer audience questions. The lectures are held at 7:00 p.m. the second Thursday of the month, and the series is hosted and moderated by a local multimedia artist whose work has been showcased in a previous program.

PANEL DISCUSSIONS OR PRESENTATIONS

Panel discussions usually involve multiple speakers and a moderator. They provide an excellent way to address specific issues and topics, to tie together disparate speakers or viewpoints, and to combine various formats, such as PowerPoint presentations, lectures, and demonstrations. Panel discussions usually involve presentations (lecture, demonstration, PowerPoint) by each panelist followed by a moderator-facilitated discussion between the panelists and often the audience. The panel discussion can be a very effective way to facilitate and add depth to the public exchange of ideas.

The Buffalo and Erie County Public Library and the Lockwood Memorial Library, State University of New York at Buffalo, collaborated on a LIVE! @ your library series on the theme of "Losing Geography" that brought back nationally recognized artists Cindy Sherman, Robert Longo, and Charles Clough, who had worked in Buffalo in the 1970s, for panel discussions and workshops along with presentations and performances by current resident artists. The series explored contributions from the visual arts to Buffalo's evolution and the impact of the community on the artists' evolution.

September 11, 2001, and subsequent anniversaries of that date have provided the catalyst for lectures and panel discussions in many libraries. For example, Hobe Sound Public Library and Cummings Library, Martin County, Florida, hosted discussions on the topic "The History and Psychology of Mideast Terrorism," featuring Indian River Community College professors Robert Farley and Joe Grisham. The professors explored the psychology of terrorism from a social-psychological perspective with a particular focus on extremism and behavior and attitudes. Discussions focused on issues related to the mindset of terrorists, the psychological impact of terrorism on the masses, cultural and religious issues, and what drives extremism.

In Rockford, Illinois, the public library partnered with the League of Women Voters of Greater Rockford to organize a panel presentation on "Coming Together in the Aftermath of the September 11 Attack." Zoe Norwood, adult services program committee chair, said the program was geared toward the political, cultural, and socioreligious issues raised by the attack. Topics included terrorism and terrorist groups, the rhetoric of war and how an enemy is constructed by leaders, American foreign policy both in history and currently, and what is Islam. The six-person panel included two political science professors, a communications professor, a sociology professor, a rabbi, and a representative of the Muslim Association of Greater Rockford. The program was two hours in length, including questions, and was moderated by the official moderator of the League of Women Voters. The format was a ten-minute opening presentation by each panelist, followed by a ten-minute period in which the panelists could pose comments or questions to each other, followed by questions from the audience using a floor microphone.

In Seattle, the University of Washington's Odegaard Undergraduate Library found that "students really had a strong desire to debrief about news information related to the attacks," according to Cassandra Hartnett, U.S. documents librarian. On October 11, 2001, the library offered a program, "Rumors, Scams, and Urban Legends Related to September 11." Audience members were asked to provide examples of September 11–related rumors they had heard, such as false Nostradamus prophecies, warnings of biological attacks through the mail, and accusations that the attacks were orchestrated by the U.S. government. Program panelists disproved rumors and offered advice to attendees on how to evaluate the validity of information they receive.

In Eugene, Oregon, the public library presented a panel discussion entitled "Keep the Dialogue Going: Perspectives on Islamic Culture and History" after community members were outraged by vandalism of the local Islamic Cultural Center.

In a partnership between the Dane County Library Service and University of Wisconsin–Madison Center for the Humanities, university faculty discussed the rights and obligations of American citizens in the aftermath of September 11 and the protections the Constitution affords in times of crisis in The Constitution Now series of five humanities forums.

The forums were held at Dane County libraries in January and February on the following topics: "The Rhetoric of a World Crisis" at Middleton Public Library, "Freedom and Democracy: Lessons from Antiquity" at Deerfield Public Library, "The Role of Civil Liberties in War Time" at Sun Prairie Public Library, "The First Amendment after September 11" at McFarland Public Library, and "Military Tribunals: National Security versus the Constitution?" at the Oregon Public Library. The organizers were Julie Chase at Dane County and Joan Strasbaugh at UW–Madison Center for the Humanities.

Participatory Discussions

BOOK DISCUSSIONS

Book Groups. Many libraries provide a home for self-sustaining book groups created by or for individuals with like tastes or interests. Members may be people with something in common, such as parents or retirees. Some groups are formed around genres, such as science fiction, romance, or classics. Libraries and librarians may be conveners, promoters, or facilitators for book discussions in or outside the library. They may provide reader's advisory assistance in selecting books and finding background materials for established or newly forming groups. They may also serve more administrative functions, such as procuring sets of books for self-organized groups via interlibrary loan or coordinating or implementing an already existing discussion group model. As they begin programming, libraries may move from offering space to preexisting or just-forming groups to creating and promoting book discussion programs for specific audiences.

Let's Talk about It. A well-established program model for book discussion series is Let's Talk about It, based on a model developed by the Vermont Humanities Council in the 1970s and launched nationally by the American Library Association in the early 1980s, with the support of the National Endowment for the Humanities. This model focuses on reading a common series of texts, chosen by a nationally known scholar, and discussing them in the context of a larger theme. Over the past twenty years, the model has been adopted—and adapted—by hundreds of libraries throughout the country.

Among ALA's themes for Let's Talk about It are

> "Individual Rights and Community in America," including Rousseau's *Social Contract* and Hawthorne's *Scarlet Letter*;
>
> "'Long Gone': The Literature and Culture of African American Migration," including the books *If He Hollers Let Him Go*, by Chester Himes, and *Devil in a Blue Dress*, by Walter Mosley;
>
> "One Vision, Many Voices: Latino Literature in the United States," including the books *Dreaming in Cuban*, by Cristina Garcia, and *In the Time of the Butterflies*, by Julia Alvarez;
>
> "Not for Children Only: Children's Classics for Adults," including E. B. White's *Charlotte's Web* and Lois Lowry's *The Giver*.

An ALA series on Jewish literature developed in 2004 included these themes and titles:

Your Heart's Desire: Sex and Love in Jewish Literature

Portnoy's Complaint, Philip Roth

Collected Stories, Grace Paley

A Simple Story, S. Y. Agnon

The Mind-Body Problem, Rebecca Goldstein

The Lover, A. B. Yehoshua

Demons, Golems, and Dybbuks: Monsters of the Jewish Imagination

The Metamorphosis, Franz Kafka

The Dybbuk, S. Ansky

Satan in Goray, I. B. Singer

The Puttermesser Papers, Cynthia Ozick

Angels in America, Tony Kushner

Between Two Worlds: Stories of Estrangement and Homecoming

Mr. Sammler's Planet, Saul Bellow

Out of Egypt, Andre Aciman

Lost in Translation, Eva Hoffman

Kaaterskill Falls, Allegra Goodman

Centaur in the Garden, Moacyr Scliar

A Mind of Her Own: Fathers and Daughters in a Changing World

Tevye the Dairyman, Sholem Aleichem

Bee Season, Myla Goldberg

American Pastoral, Philip Roth

Bread Givers, Anzia Yierzeska

1185 Park Avenue: A Memoir, Anne Roiphe

In the last decade, Let's Talk about It has been promoted primarily by state humanities councils, which have produced regional themes and offered libraries grants to pay local scholars to present and facilitate the programs. Often state humanities councils provide publicity and program materials, such as printed brochures that highlight the theme in each of the books to be discussed, for the local scholar-leader to use to frame discussion and/or for participants to read on their own as background. Some councils also track the libraries in the state that have used various themes and may have sets of books to loan. Most can help libraries locate an appropriate scholar.

The following themes, developed by the Maine Humanities Council, Maine Center for the Book, and Maine State Library, illustrate the richness of available material:

"Crossing Over: Mediating between Cultures in Contemporary American Indian Literature," focusing on works by James Welch, Leslie Marmon Silko, Louise Erdrich, Sherman Alexie, and Louis Owens

"Exploring Human Boundaries: Literary Perspectives on Health Care Providers and Their Patients," including *The Spirit Catches You and You Fall Down*, by Anne Fadiman, *The Plague*, by Albert Camus, and *Wit*, by Margaret Edson

"The Mirror of Maine: The Maine Community in Myth and Reality," featuring works by Stephen King and other Maine residents

The National Endowment for the Humanities (NEH) has been the major national funder of Let's Talk about It since 1983, and, in 1992, NEH program officer Tom Phelps wrote, "For nearly ten years the project has brought people together in this nation's libraries to talk about important themes found in great literature and history. It has influenced thousands of American citizens and has challenged nearly as many public librarians to consider the importance of their library's educational mission." Phelps continued, "Reading and discussion programs in every state, territory and district . . . emerged as a result of the Let's Talk about It project. From the original 5 themes, 234 (and probably more) have been born. . . . More than six thousand libraries have participated in projects that follow the Let's Talk about It model."

One Community, One Book. Another model that has gained tremendous popularity is the One Community, One Book model, in which the library, as the leader of a cooperative of community and cultural organizations, promotes the reading of a single title by all members of the community at a common time. At last count, more than 150 communities large and small in 45 states had implemented this program, first presented in 1998 in Seattle. In addition to the one-on-one dialogue that happens serendipitously when so many are reading the same book—whether *A Lesson before Dying, To Kill a Mockingbird,* or *Fahrenheit 451*—communities plan a number of formal book discussions at various venues; lectures and panel discussions on the book, its themes, or the author; and related presentations (such as a mock trial in the case of *Mockingbird*). Frequently, the program culminates in a visit by the author, complete with interviews, receptions, and readings. For those planning a One Book event, the American Library Association's ALA Graphics offers a graphic arts CD that contains templates and tools for promotional and marketing materials, as well as a how-to guide and a toolkit produced by the ALA Public Programs Office. The how-to guide, "Planning Your Community-Wide Read," is also downloadable as a PDF (Portable Document File) through the ALA Public Programs Office Online Resource Center at http://www.ala.org/publicprograms/orc/.

VIEWING OR LISTENING AND DISCUSSION PROGRAMS

Expanding beyond book discussion programs to other media has been popular for at least the last decade. Film and audio programs offer equal fodder for information, discussion, and debate.

At the forefront is National Video Resources (http://www.nvr.org/), which offers thematic packages on such topics as "Fast Forward: Technology and the Communications Revolution" and "Presidents, Politics, and Power: American Presidents Who Shaped the 20th Century," materials, and grants, as well as advice regarding developing film and video collections and using film in programming.

The Ann Arbor (Mich.) District Library is one of many libraries that created a thematic series linking NVR's film series From Rosie to Roosevelt: The American People with additional programs and exhibits on World War II. The NVR series includes the films *The Home Front, The*

Life and Times of Rosie the Riveter, *Color of Honor*, *Days of Waiting*, *Proudly We Served: The Men of the USS Mason*, *America and the Holocaust: Deceit and Indifference*, and *D-Day*.

Some libraries host screenings and discussions of major PBS series specials, especially those by Ken Burns, Bill Moyers, and *P.O.V.*, which offer high-interest and timely topics for discussion.

A precursor to NVR's film programming was library programs using videos from the Annenberg/CPB series on modern poetry *Voices and Visions*, featuring such poets as Emily Dickinson, William Carlos Williams, and Langston Hughes. Libraries presented thematic subsets of the thirteen-part series (usually four to five poets), along with printed discussion materials and programs facilitated by local scholars.

A later audio series, *Poets in Person*, produced by the Modern Poetry Association and broadcast on National Public Radio, featured thirteen half-hour programs, each on a single living poet—including Sharon Olds, Rita Dove, A. R. Ammons, and Gary Soto. The audio programs featured biographical material about and readings by these engaging and influential writers, as well as conversations with fellow poets and scholars about their work and critical commentary. Libraries distribute audiotapes of the programs and a paperback listener's guide to participants who come to the library for scholar-facilitated discussion.

DISCUSSION PROGRAMS FOR NEW AND DEVELOPING READERS

Many libraries have presented program models designed especially for people with low literacy skills to create opportunities for them to participate in reading and discussion. Among these are the Prime Time Family Reading Time model of the Louisiana Endowment for the Humanities and Connections by the Vermont Humanities Council.

Prime Time Family Reading Time. Prime Time is a six- or eight-week reading, discussion, and storytelling program in which a university scholar (who functions as a discussion leader) and a storyteller conduct weekly book discussions and storytelling sessions based on award-winning children's books. Prime Time reinforces the role of the family as a major social and economic unit. It trains parents and children to bond around the act of reading and learning together to improve skills and achievements. It teaches parents and children to read and discuss humanities topics (history, literature, and ethical issues, such as fairness, greed, honor, and deceit) as a way of fostering high academic expectations and achievements in low-literacy, low-income families. It encourages low-literacy, low-income parents to enter or continue their own educational programs, whether GED or other training, and enter the workforce, and it helps parents and children learn how to select books and become active library users. For more information about Prime Time, visit http://www.leh.org/.

Connections. Vermont's Connections book-discussion programs serve adult literacy students, at-risk middle-school and high-school students, Head Start and Even Start parents, correctional inmates, teen parents, people learning English as a second language, and others developing their reading skills. Connections programs help participants develop the skills and motivation to read and to enjoy reading as well as the confidence to talk about books and ideas. Participants keep the books free of charge in order to build their own home libraries. The programs provide both quality reading material and the social interaction with books that is crucial to developing a love of reading and ideas. Each Connections series consists of three sessions, two to four weeks apart, and most sessions use three books. Discussion leaders are encouraged to tailor the series to their audience by developing writing components and other activities to accompany each series. Sample themes include "Heroes," "Friendship," and "The Call of Ancient Stories." For more information, visit http://www.vermonthumanities.org/.

OTHER PACKAGED READING AND DISCUSSION PROGRAMS

A number of models for public policy discussion programs exist, including

> Choices for the 21st Century, from Brown University (http://www.watsoninstitute.org/);

> National Issues Forums, from the Kettering Foundation (http://www.nifi.org/);

> Study Circles (http://www.studycircles.org/).

These sources offer program models, discussion materials, and guidance in presenting and facilitating programs.

DISCUSSIONS RELATED TO PERFORMANCES

In cooperation with the Lyric Opera of Chicago, the suburban Highland Park (Ill.) Public Library presents the Lyric Opera Lecture Series featuring local scholars presenting programs about upcoming opera performances.

Performances

MUSICAL PERFORMANCES

For libraries that have the space and acoustics (or can collaborate with a group that does) musical performances can tap into many new audiences. The following examples of library programs show the range of music genres.

The Bismarck-Mandan Symphony Orchestra in North Dakota collaborated with the library to present a series of concerts and lectures.

Spoken-word artist Sekou Sundiata appeared with a six-piece band in programs at the public library in Washington, DC.

Old Sounds in New Lands: A Celebration of Kentucky's Appalachian Music was a series of lectures and musical performances exploring the music brought to the Appalachian region by early immigrants. Sponsored by the Eastern Kentucky University Libraries, the series featured performances by folksinger Jean Ritchie, lectures and performances by the Scots-Irish music ensemble Pale, Stout and Amber, and lectures by Dr. Ron Pen, director of the John Jacob Niles Center for American Music, and Homer Ledford, a dulcimer maker and bluegrass specialist.

University of California–San Diego Arts Libraries presented The Art of Surfing, a multiarts series combining lectures, films, and artifacts, and featuring a musical performance and presentation by Dick Dale, "the Father of Surf Guitar."

San Jose (Calif.) Public Library presented a six-month series of multiarts programs that included author presentations by Gary Soto, lectures and activities by muralist Pilar Aguero and author/illustrator Bobbi Salinas, performances by singer Joe Silva, readings by poet Chitra Divakaruni, dance performances by the Payal Dance Troupe, and a reading and dialogue with novelist Rudolfo Anaya.

King County (Wash.) Library System's Voices from the Rim series celebrated the authors and arts of the Pacific Rim. This multiarts series of performances incorporated activities and presentations for all age groups: performances by the Japanese-American taiko drum group Kaze Daiko, traditional hula music, dance and drama, Japanese folktales, sumi-e brush painting lessons, and readings by authors Ha Jin, Lois-Ann Yamanaka, Molly Gloss, Brenda Peterson, Philip Red Eagle, and Lydia Minatoya. King County's ambitious series successfully blended the presentation of multiple art forms to a wide variety of audiences with sustained focus on a specific theme.

The Fairfax County Public Library in Virginia worked with a local orchestra to present separate concerts celebrating the heritages of two significant groups in the community, Koreans and Hispanics.

In a memorable event at an American Library Association Midwinter Meeting, Paul Burch and the WPA Ballclub performed as part of ALA President Nancy Kranich's program based on the theme "Libraries: The Cornerstone of Democracy." Burch composed and performed an original song for the occasion, "Democracy Rag, Whine, and Blues," and the band performed songs inspired by fellow Nashvillian Tony Early's best-selling novel *Jim the Boy*.

DRAMATIC PERFORMANCES

Dramatic performances can draw new audiences much as musical performances do. For example, Queens Borough (N.Y.) Public Library Jackson Heights Branch explored the LIVE! @ your library theme of "Losing Geography, Discovering Self" by presenting two Immigrants' Theater Project productions: *I Love America*, Lidia Romirez's play depicting the stories of eleven female immigrants from the Dominican Republic and Puerto Rico, and Alvin Eng's *Flushing Cycle*, a memoir monologue about the playwright's unusual odyssey from the Flushing of his childhood, where he was one of only a few Chinese children, to the Flushing of today, where he is one of the few Chinese who do not speak fluent Chinese.

The San Diego Public Library presented six performances of *Glass Cord*, a play written and directed by Evelyn Diaz Cruz, an adjunct professor at California State University. Two playwriting workshops conducted by the playwright were also offered in the library's City Heights Urban Village Performance Annex.

Exhibitions

A library can develop exhibitions drawn from local library or community collections and ideas. Libraries can also rent or apply for traveling exhibitions constructed by national, regional, or local organizations.

An exhibit is not a program per se, but much like a book, film, or performance, its theme can provide a springboard to related programming. For example, a photographic exhibition on homelessness by a local photographer might be accompanied by a series of programs—a workshop on taking and developing photographs, a lecture by the photographer on the themes and aims of her work, and a panel discussion on community responses to homelessness.

Exhibitions in libraries stimulate the public's interest in the world of ideas. They are not ends in themselves but starting points for substantive programming, discussion, and study. Think of an exhibition as a theme or framework for related programming.

LOCALLY BASED EXHIBITIONS

A good example of a locally developed exhibit is the collaboration by the Greenwich (Conn.) Library with the United Way of Greenwich and the Urban Artists Initiative to present Portals of Change, a two-day cultural symposium built around an architectural sculpture installation by Stamford artist Shaw Stuart. Two days of events on the theme of "Changing Communities" celebrated ancient and contemporary cultures through many different program formats, including a conversation with the artist, Peruvian musical performances, lectures on Greek history and mythology, a children's arts workshop, classical Indian dance performances, discussion panels, and poetry readings and slams.

TRAVELING EXHIBITIONS

One goal of American Library Association–sponsored exhibitions is to encourage visitors to go beyond the images to explore the exhibitions' themes in other areas of a library's collections. This is accomplished through related programs and bibliographic aids developed and offered by host libraries. A related goal is to help libraries strengthen their role as intellectual forums and central cultural and educational institutions in their communities.

Among the touring exhibitions that have been sponsored by the American Library Association are *The Many Realms of King Arthur*, *Frankenstein: Penetrating the Secrets of Nature*, *Beyond Category: The Musical Genius of Duke Ellington*, *Listening to the Prairie*, *Go Figure!* and *The Frontier in American Culture*. Examples of programming associated with these exhibitions can be found in chapter 4, throughout this chapter, and in the appendix.

Most ALA traveling exhibitions are available by application. See the ALA Public Programs Office website (http://www.ala.org/public programs/) for current information.

Other sources for rental traveling exhibitions include

> Smithsonian Institution Traveling Exhibition Service (SITES); (http://www.sites.si.edu/)
>
> Harry Ransom Research Center, University of Texas at Austin (http://www.hrc.utexas.edu/exhibitions/traveling/)
>
> Exhibits USA (http://www.maaa.org/exhi_usa/)
>
> Blair-Murrah Exhibitions (http://blair-murrah.org/)
>
> Library of the Jewish Theological Seminary (http://www.jtsa.edu/library/exhib/trav/index.shtml/)

Children's museums, galleries, cultural and heritage museums, and state and regional arts and humanities councils are also sources for traveling exhibitions.

Book Festivals

These often massive, populist literary events are usually held at the city, state, or regional levels and often last a few days, usually over a weekend. Because book festivals contain such broad program offerings over a relatively short period of time, their planning and execution often involve one or more sponsoring organization and dozens of programming and marketing partners. For example, the Southern Kentucky Book Fest is presented by Western Kentucky University Libraries/Kentucky Museum, Bowling Green Public Library and Barnes and Noble Booksellers. Because of their exceptionally large attendance figures (ranging from a thousand to five hundred thousand people), book festivals usually have equally large mission statements and goals, such as "to encourage reading and the love of books and to be a positive force in reducing the illiteracy in our region and state" (Bowling Green Public Library) or "to promote reading, encourage writing, and heighten an awareness of literacy and the literary arts in our multiethnic community" (Miami Book Fair International) or "to celebrate books and the joy of reading" (National Book Festival). Among the best known are the Miami Book Fair International, the Southern Festival of Books in Nashville, New York Is Book Country, and the Los Angeles Times Festival of Books. Others include the Wisconsin Book Festival in Madison, the South Carolina Book Festival, the Border Book Festival in southern New Mexico, the Vegas Valley Book Festival (a cooperative effort of the Nevada Humanities Committee, Henderson District Public Libraries, and the City of Henderson Department of Parks and Recreation), the West Virginia Book Festival, and the Virginia Festival of the Book—VABook!

Typical elements of book festivals are readings and panel discussions; book sales and signings; exhibit booths featuring booksellers, publishers, and related organizations; and children's events, such as book-related crafts and activities, storytellers, puppet shows, and costumed book characters. Some book festivals also include special events such as musical performances, usually with a literary tie-in, or exhibits or demonstrations in the book and paper arts. The Southern Festival of Books in Nashville presents a Café Stage featuring talented Nashville singers, songwriters, and poets and a Theater Stage featuring local actors and playwrights. Many also include writing or getting-published workshops, panels, and contests. Some festivals present literary awards or undertake other activities to recognize authors and publishers. Kanawha County Public Library does its annual used-book sale on the first day of the two-day West Virginia Book Festival, sponsored by the Library Foundation of Kanawha County, Inc., and the West Virginia Humanities Council.

Laura Bush created a National Book Festival with the Library of Congress, based on the success she had as the impetus for the annual Texas Book Festival in Austin, where proceeds from the sale of books and merchandise benefit public libraries in Texas.

Libraries may have a central role as sponsor, planner and programmer, or convener. They frequently serve as venues for events. Many festivals also look to partnering literary organizations, including libraries, to develop and present programs. The Arizona Book Festival is sponsored by the Arizona Humanities Council, the Maricopa County Library District, and the Arizona State Library and is held at the Carnegie Library Park/

Arizona State Library in Phoenix. The humanities council awards contracts worth from $1,000 to $2,000 to organizations to present literary programs at the festival.

At the Southern Festival of Books, talks, readings, and panel discussions occur in rooms under War Memorial Plaza, in the state capitol building, and in the Nashville Public Library, which are all adjacent to one another.

Organizing or affiliated agencies will sometimes offer meetings or related training opportunities for librarians. These occasions are also good sources for librarians seeking presenters for future events.

Themes: More Than a Title

Many of the preceding examples reflect series tied together thematically as well as by format. Themes are intended to focus your programs on topics, issues, and ideas that are important to your community. Choosing a theme helps you identify local issues, as well as look for authors and artists whose works address those issues. Themes are a way to articulate your program goals and communicate them to your audience and your presenters. When chosen carefully, themes can help shape your planning, provide variety and breadth, and strengthen and deepen the impact of your programs.

LIVE! Themes

Figure 5-1 shows themes developed for the American Library Association's LIVE! @ your library initiative, linking themes, discussion, and content ideas with related programming/collaboration ideas. Some libraries have found innovative ways to build on the themes. For example, the University Library of Indiana/Purdue University chose "Other People's Stories: The Art of Biography" as the theme for a tribute to Louis Armstrong, whose life story was told through a performance by a vocal and instrumental jazz ensemble. The program was presented to coincide with a local jazz festival.

Working with the theme "In the Current" to examine ways of resolving community violence, the Salina Public Library in Kansas developed a series of programs for artists-in-residence Tim Rollins and D. C. Cornish to work with at-risk young adults in the community. Partners included the Salina Art Center and Salina Human Relations Department.

The Douglas (Colo.) Public Library District presented a four-part family poetry series themed "It's All Relative." At four branch libraries, patrons heard a reading by notable poet Brad Bowles and were led in playful poetry-writing exercises. "Families left with their own newly written poems and fresh ideas for poetry in their everyday lives."

The Montclair (N.J.) Public Library built on the theme "Making Change" by presenting a series of events with the general title "Transgender Stories, Transgender Lives." Included were a film screening and scholar-led discussion of *A Boy Named Sue*, presentations and readings by authors and transgender activists Leslie Feinberg and Minnie Bruce Pratt, and a discussion forum on and for transgender youth and their families.

FIGURE 5-1 LIVE! @ your library Sample Themes

Theme	Description/Questions	Related Program/ Collaboration Ideas
Losing Geography, Discovering Self	Migration, immigration, and displacement can all lead to the discovery of self in art and literature. What communities are in transition in terms of culture? How do individuals and groups cope in new environments? How does a changing landscape require the search for a new identity? How does the artist create when confronted with new borders and boundaries?	Pair authors and artists who were born or once lived in your region with those from other countries/cultures who live there now or who represent current population groups; explore real and imagined landscapes in art, music, and literature; use art to claim space, explore nature, protest loss.
Body and Soul	Examine the relationships between physical, mental, and spiritual well-being, especially as explored by authors and artists whose work illuminates illness, loss, and the struggle or triumph of the spirit. How have artists been affected by or responded to AIDS, cancer, depression, and other illnesses? What are the limits of human life, as explored in science and fiction? Can words, images, and characters help heal the individual and the community?	Work with local health-care organizations to exhibit and feature work by people with illnesses or disabilities; hold benefit readings for cancer, AIDS, or other causes; mail program information to membership groups with related program interests.
In the Current	Authors and artists are commentators on everything from the Internet to the human genome to reducing violence. Comparing and contrasting responses, especially on controversial topics, can be a way to explore issues that might be hard to take on more directly. Mixing fiction and nonfiction, hip-hop and classical music, photography and abstract art offers multiple approaches to attract and engage varied audiences.	Compare the treatment of issues on the page to their treatment on screen and airwaves: Is there a difference in impact, in glorifying versus analyzing? Develop programs that feature filmmakers, recording artists, journalists, mystery writers; partner with schools and issue-oriented community groups.
Making Change	Characters in fiction, poetry, and art offer political and personal responses to an incredible range of social issues, from racism to running for office, homelessness to hate crimes. What do we learn about real life from characters reshaping their fictional worlds? How does literature mirror contemporary reality in cities, small towns, workplaces? How do research and news events play into fiction and poetry?	Present a musical program of protest songs from the 1960s; organize an antiwar film series; coordinate panel discussions with local community leaders and organizations on issues explored in the works of presenting artists.

Theme	Description/Questions	Related Program/ Collaboration Ideas
It's All Relative: Families in Art and Literature	Just as artists draw on their own family experiences, audiences bring their own history and memory to reading and viewing stories about family. What incidents or events shape one's family? How do we use language and images to embrace memory? How do other families, real or imagined, help us understand our own?	Feature writers and artists of different generations; explore the roles of families in different cultures; offer a reading and discussion series on families in contemporary literature; use anthologies that explore families, young writers, cross-cultural themes.
Additional Sample Themes	Playing Ball with Words: Sports and the Arts Other People's Stories: The Art of Biography Fighting Words: Writing about War and Peace	

Emmy-Award-winning filmmaker David Grubin spoke at the Enoch Pratt Free Library in Baltimore, Maryland, on the theme of "Other People's Stories: The Art of Biography."

The Lexington (Ky.) Public Library held a four-event series on the theme "Playing Ball with Words," featuring award-winning young adult novelist Chris Crutcher and local writers and poets. The library partnered with the YMCA, the Kentucky Writers Coalition, and a local youth center to target the programs to youth audiences.

Princeton Public Library in New Jersey, in collaboration with the Arts Council of Princeton and Princeton High School, presented a series on the theme "Losing Geography" that included a poetry reading and jazz performance by Pulitzer Prize–winning poet Yusef Komunyakaa and Jazz Ensemble; a slide show on Jacob Lawrence's landmark Migration series; and a residency with author Julia Alvarez. Additional partners included two area universities, the state humanities council, and a local film society.

Tie-Ins

Opportunities for tie-ins abound, from National Library Week, National Poetry Month, and Jazz Appreciation Month (all in April) to Banned Books Week, Teen Read Week, Women's History Month, Black History Month, Gay/Lesbian History Month, and local events. *Chase's Calendar of Events* (McGraw-Hill/Contemporary Books, annual) is a good compendium of observances.

CHAPTER 6

The Talent
and Showtime

Without culture, and the relative freedom it implies, society, even when perfect, is but a jungle. This is why any authentic creation is a gift to the future. —ALBERT CAMUS

Program Presenters and Where to Find Them

Who They Are and What They Do

You will probably work with a wide variety of program presenters if you do programming for any length of time. Many presenters fall into more than one category. For example, the university English professor who is also a published fiction writer may be called on to lead a book discussion series one year, conduct a creative writing workshop the next year, and perform a reading of her short fiction the next. Some programs will also encompass more than one category, such as a poetry reading accompanied by music or the opening of an art exhibition that features the artist and a critic.

Among the talent you may work with will be those who self-identify in many different ways: poets, fiction writers (novelists, short-story writers, genre writers, graphic novelists, and comic book writers), nonfiction writers, journalists, dramatists/playwrights, screenwriters, professors (of literature, creative writing, history, philosophy, area studies, music, dance, art, art history), singers, musicians, bands or orchestras, dancers, dance companies, theater companies, chautauqua (or living-history) performers, actors, performance artists, and visual artists such as painters, photographers, sculptors, printmakers, fiber artists, filmmakers, and online artists. You may ask them to perform or demonstrate their work; talk about their work; instruct others in the art, techniques, and business of their work; or talk about or facilitate discussion about the work of others.

What Is in It for Them?

Presenters are not likely to become rich and famous by working with libraries. However, there are a number of reasons they may wish to be exposed to library audiences. The chief reasons are:

> In general, library audiences are appreciative and well prepared. They bring ideas and life experiences to the programs that enrich all concerned. They are open-minded and willing to be responsive to work in progress. Presenters usually learn as much as they teach.

> By and large the presenter does get paid (and some presenters sell books or CDs).

> Many presenters go on to become rich and famous, or at least widely recognized for their work, and tend to look back fondly on the ways in which libraries recognized and supported them during their emerging years.

> Many adults, especially writers, have very positive experiences with libraries.

The comments in box 6-1 offer insight into how presenters feel about libraries and library audiences.

Seeking/Evaluating Potential Presenters

When seeking appropriate presenters, you are looking for two basic things: (1) credentials and quality of work and (2) professionalism, ease, and authority with adult audiences. You are looking for a person who has something excellent to offer and can effectively express it.

QUOTES FROM PRESENTERS

Most writers have a relationship with the page and long for the oral dimension lost in our culture. The act of reading can be nurtured, developed, heightened. That's what a good library can do, and that's what bringing a writer into the library can contribute. It's good for the reader to see . . . that the book and the writer are not the same.

—Stuart Dybek, Writers Live at the Library presenter

As a writer, it is seldom or ever that I get a chance to communicate directly (eye to eye) with the people who have either read or are familiar with my work—they know more about me than I know about them. It is a chance to "test fly" work in progress.

—Larry Heinemann, Writers Live at the Library presenter

I was impressed by the dedication of those who came to that session—they asked good questions and offered really worthwhile interpretations. . . . The group tackled [the book's] difficulties with considerable energy. . . . The discussion was lively, the evening a success.

—Let's Talk about It series scholar/ discussion facilitator

What a great joy it has been to share stories with writers, librarians, and readers in the wonderful sites that I have visited.

—Denise Chávez, LIVE! @ your library presenter

Love giving library presentations. It gets an interesting group of people together.

—Chris Crutcher, LIVE! @ your library presenter

It's important that writers not be seen only as outsiders who drop in for a spell through their art, with concerns that matter to people in the community.

—Scott Russell Sanders, LIVE! @ your library presenter

To some degree you will have to develop your own criteria. However, it is usually easier to evaluate credentials than to assess appropriateness for your audience. For example, you may look at a fiction writer's publications and how well they have been reviewed. You may seek a PhD in a particular field for a lecture or to facilitate a discussion. You may review a musical group's performances or CDs or its members' formal training in music. When you are interested in a presenter who has no easily identified degrees, publication history, reviews, or the like, you may need to develop other approaches. For example, you might pair an established, published poet with a new poet who has only one or two published poems, especially if the established poet has mentored the newer poet or admires that person's work.

The ability to create an artistic or scholarly work or to develop expertise in an area is one thing. The ability to present that work or expertise to an audience is another. There will always be the stereotypical shy and nervous or droning and pompous presenters, as well as the awkward or unpleasant, the chronically late, and the no-shows. Though truly troublesome presenters are atypical, they do exist. More typical are those whose work is exemplary but whose public presentation skills are not—due either to temperament or to lack of experience. Your job is to determine that the presenter has both the experience and the ability to deliver your program.

Word of mouth and personal observation are some of the best ways to determine the suitability of a given performer or presenter. Get referrals from people you trust, observe the person in action, if possible, and ask lots of questions. Is the person comfortable with an adult audience? Is she aware of who the audience is? Can she relate to, create a rapport with, or make her work clear to the audience? Is her presentation informative, entertaining, provocative, exciting, enlightening, or insightful?

Sometimes the source recommending a potential presenter can provide the most helpful information about their suitability. Talk with the presenter, the publicist or agent handling the presenter, other libraries, bookstores, and organizations the presenter has worked with in the past. If possible, communicate directly with the presenter about your expectations for the program (see "Hiring and Working with Presenters," later in this chapter).

Another consideration is programming balance, particularly in cases where issues may be of a political, religious, or other sensitive nature. Will the presenter be impartial or be appropriately broad-minded? Or will one presenter's viewpoints be balanced by the viewpoints of other presenters?

Program presenters can be found in many ways, as illustrated by the partial listing of suggested sources in box 6-2. Most libraries find that once cultural programming is begun, word travels fast—successful presenters recommend other presenters, and community members seek out the library with suggestions.

BOX 6-2

SOURCES FOR PRESENTERS

Recommendations from colleagues locally and through wider professional networks

Recommendations from community members or partner organizations

Programs presented by other entities in your community or by libraries or other cultural organizations in other communities

Relevant departments of local universities and community colleges

State and regional library, book, arts, and humanities agencies

Local chapters of national organizations: League of Women Voters, Rotary, Veterans of Foreign Wars, American Civil Liberties Union, Jewish Community Centers, religious and political groups, and American Association of University Women

Directories such as Poets and Writers' *Directory of American Poets and Fiction Writers* (available in print or online) and the Authors @ your library database

Literary organizations such as the Academy of American Poets, Associated Writing Programs, New York City's 92nd St. Y, Poets House, the

Loft Literary Center in Minneapolis, Chicago's Guild Complex, Seattle Arts and Lectures, and Literary Arts, Inc., in Portland, Oregon

Lists and recommendations of best books from sources such as ALA's *Booklist* and annual notable books lists

Arts and humanities organizations such as Americans for the Arts, Art in the Public Interest, Arts Midwest, National Alliance for Media Arts and Culture, National Video Resources, Western States Arts Federation, and National Humanities Alliance

Publishers (especially such smaller literary presses as BOA Editions, Copper Canyon Press, Milkweed Editions, Sarabande Books, Tia Chuca Press, and Arte Publico Press), producers, and distributors

Showcases, conferences, and other special events featuring potential presenters

Book festivals and other specialist events

Referrals from national organizations such as the American Library Association Public Programs Office rosters and model programs

Unpublished and Self-Published Authors

Experienced programmers sometimes have the challenge of choosing among and fending off too many potential programs and suggestions. Local unpublished or self-published authors may be especially eager to increase their visibility. One experienced programmer offers the following advice for dealing with such authors:

> I get more requests for signings by unknown authors than I can accommodate, and if I haven't seen the book or favorable reviews from sources I trust, I generally just say we don't have the staff time to host and publicize a program for them and that attendance at such events is generally disappointing, both of which are true.
>
> I don't want to box myself in by publishing a lot of guidelines for decisions of this sort. I could say I must see three favorable reviews of a book in reputable sources, for example, and then find myself in lots of arguments about what "favorable" and "reputable" mean and how I picked the number three. I will say that local authors and topics of local interest have high priority on the time I can give to programs.
>
> Publishers' names and reviews still count for a lot in evaluating the quality and interest of a book. Promotional materials tell a lot about the quality of the product. Many books of local interest are self-published, and for that and other reasons I would not make a rule against hosting events promoting self-published books. However, I see a lot of self-published authors who do not understand that their writing or format needs a lot more work, or that the book they have written will not sell outside

their immediate circle of friends and family. Those are not the kinds of authors I want to spend time promoting. I also don't want to gratuitously rain on their parades.

I expect this is why publishers return unsolicited manuscripts with that maddening, noncommittal form letter—"Thank you for your recent submission. We are sorry to say it does not meet our needs at this time."

In years where I have had more local authors than I could handle individually, I have thrown an open house in December and invited all local authors to show up and sell their books and give readings. They like this a lot, but I can't say it draws a lot of people besides the authors themselves and their best friends.

When approached by potential presenters, their fans, or their agents, a good first step is to ask to see copies of their books or other work, biographies, and relevant reviews, articles, and links to websites. The material may not fit into current or future plans, or it may open up a new realm of ideas. Always be open-minded and consider material on a case-by-case basis. And be prepared to innovate or to revisit decisions in the future. You may find yourself ahead of the curve on the next big thing.

Hiring and Working with Presenters

Once you have identified a desired presenter, there are several steps to securing an appearance.

Talk It Out; Then Get It in Writing

After an initial discussion in which you and the presenter discuss the scope of activity and specifically what you want the presenter to do, it is advisable to put down in writing—often in letter format—the details of what you have agreed, with all relevant dates, fees, and requirements of both parties. You can ask the presenter to sign and return a copy of the letter as confirmation. Some presenters will require a more formal contract, which may be handled by an agent, publicist, or other intermediary.

Details to cover in the presenter's contract or letter of confirmation may include

- Time, date, and location
- Program format
- Venue capacity
- Transportation and lodging arrangements
- Fees
- Introductions
- Book sales and autographing arrangements
- On-site contact person
- Required audiovisual support
- Request for publicity materials, presenter's head shot, press release, and advance copy of book
- Special needs

Publicity and Marketing Materials

You will want to ask the presenter to provide up-to-date biographical or other background material, including photos, to use in your publicity. If this has already been gathered as part of your selection process, you may simply want to ask that the presenter review materials you prepare or confirm that what you have is accurate. Some presenters or their publicists can provide their own mailing lists or have access to specific media. Let them help you ensure an audience.

Hospitality and Local Arrangements

If the presenter is not local, you will need to make arrangements for transportation, lodging, and meals in connection with the appearance. Details of the arrangements should be thoroughly discussed with the presenter in advance. For example, although some presenters may happily lodge as guests in personal residences, many will prefer the privacy and quiet of a hotel or motel. Members of your planning team or others may vie for the opportunity to meet the visitor at the airport or provide a tour of the area. (Again, first confirm with the presenter the desirability of such arrangements.) Local presenters may appreciate a meal with a small group before or after the presentation. Be clear about the range of expenses you can and are willing to cover, and ask about special needs or requests. Always treat the presenter as an honored guest.

Venues

Most libraries prefer to present programs on-site for a variety of reasons:

- Proximity to collections or materials participants may find of interest
- Drawing potential new users to the library space
- Showing off—or showing need for—library facilities

However, there are also good reasons for moving programs off-site:

- Reaching a desired audience on their more comfortable home turf
- Lack of suitable library facilities (such as inadequate seating capacity)
- Increasing the library's visibility among nonusers

Setting the Scene

If you have carefully planned your event, you will have everything organized and will have enlisted volunteers and staff to check all the details. On the day of the event, you will want to reconfirm specifics with the presenter (date, time, exact location, any other arrangements); check signage, room preparations, refreshments, sign-in sheets, and name-tag supplies; check with desk staff and people who answer the phone and update the website; and confirm the logistics of ticketing, seating, or other procedures. Just before the program, meet with the presenter and with volunteers, and be sure that volunteers are on hand to greet participants as they arrive.

Introductions

Introductions are an important element of the program. You or your designated volunteer should be prepared to set a positive and welcoming tone and to present an informative and enthusiastic opening for your presenter. A few suggestions:

> Be prepared with written notes, but avoid appearing to read from notes.
>
> Thank all who are responsible: the presenter and participants for coming, funders and partners for their roles, library board and staff for their work and support, and any other people deserving of recognition for their contributions.
>
> Be passionate and knowledgeable about the work of the presenter and the content of the program.
>
> Provide accurate and thoughtful information about the presenter and the content of the program. Include the presenter's name, title, and institution or group, if applicable, and a summary of the individual's most important and relevant credentials, achievements, awards, and accolades. If appropriate, a personal anecdote or other interesting tidbit will warm the audience's attitude toward the presenter.
>
> Be brief! Do not overshadow the program! And lead the applause to welcome the presenter.

The Show

Be sure someone is counting heads and distributing evaluation forms. Then relax and enjoy the program. This is your payoff.

Following Up

You can never say thank you enough. At the end of the event, make a few summarizing comments; give a pitch for the next program in the series; explain the procedure for book signing, if appropriate; entreat audience members to complete evaluations; and address any other necessities. Thank the presenter, the funders, the audience, and the helpers—staff, Friends, and everyone else.

Be sure the presenter's hospitality needs have been met and then, before you forget, jot a few notes to yourself about what went through your mind during the event. What was the most surprising thing? What would you do differently next time? What did you need to do that you had not planned? Think about the content as well as the logistics, the audience's reactions as well as the presentation or discussion.

Presenters are human. Make sure they feel that their work is appreciated by doing your best work to get a good audience. No presenter wants to face a small, halfhearted, or uncomprehending audience. Make sure presenters are paid, fed, and sincerely thanked. Treat them well and good word of mouth about you and your library will quickly spread among other potential presenters.

Listening to the Prairie

Exhibition & Events at the
Glendale Public Library

Glendale Public Library, Glendale, Arizona

CHAPTER 7

Funding for
Cultural Programs

*What do we, as a nation, care about books?
How much do you think we spend altogether
on our libraries, public or private, as compared with what we spend on our horses?*
— JOHN RUSKIN

Before you can raise money, you have to make your case. This is true whether you are working through the library's regular budget cycle or writing a grant proposal. To review some of the reasons that libraries use to justify offering cultural programming, see chapter 1.

Many sources of funds for cultural programs exist: the library budget, in-kind donations, and fund-raising. Outside sources include corporate sponsors and government, foundation, and individual donors. In recent years, the climate has been good for outside fund-raising because libraries tend to have resources to bring to bear, enjoy good track records, and are recognized as places where many issues can be addressed.

Organizational Support

Before any money can be raised or allocated, organizational support is essential. If your board, staff, and community members are not behind you, the road will be tough. The ALA survey of cultural programming at public libraries indicated that approximately 60 percent of management, staff, and board members have at least a moderate commitment to cultural programming at libraries, with about a quarter of board and staff members and a third of managers strongly committed (ALA/PPO 1999a, 12). Whether or not your library administration and board share such commitment, building a strong case is good preparation for attracting funders, developing convincing promotional materials, and keeping yourself on track. You must have your own passion and commitment, but you must also be able to collect evidence and organize information that support your ideas.

Funding from the Library Budget

The library budget is one source of funding for programming, and most funders will expect at least some matching support from the library, even if it is only in-kind. According to the 1998 survey, one out of four libraries has a separate line item in the budget for adult programming (24.1 percent). The adult programming budget is combined with children's programming in 15.8 percent of libraries. No separate line item for programming was reported by 60.2 percent of libraries. For those with a separate line item, 55.5 percent reported that compared with the previous year, the budget had stayed the same, while 36.6 percent reported an increase and 7.9 percent reported a decrease (p. 10).

Outside Sources of Funding

The library Friends group was the most frequent source of outside funding for adult programming (67.7 percent). Only 7.7 percent of libraries depended solely on library operating funds for adult programming activities in 1997. Nearly half of libraries used one or two funding sources outside their own budgets. Besides Friends, other funders included

Humanities council	31.3%
Local/state arts councils	26.9%
Local service/civic groups	19.7%
Individual donors	15.0%
Other	13.7%
Corporations/businesses	13.3%
Library foundation	10.4%
Community or local foundations	8.9%
Library Services and Technology Act/ Library Services and Constuction Act grants	5.9%
Other state government sources	5.1%
National foundations	4.9%
Other federal government sources	2.1% (p. 10)

State and National Funding Sources

State humanities and arts councils were the most frequent funders after Friends groups, whereas national agencies tended to fund regional or national projects. Major funding sources for cultural programming at the state and national levels include

National Endowment for the Humanities
(http://www.neh.gov/)

State Humanities Councils
(http://www.statehumanities.com/)

National Endowment for the Arts
(http://www.arts.endow.gov/)

National Assembly of State Arts Agencies (NASAA)
(http://www.nasaa-arts.org/)

Institute of Museum and Library Services
(http://www.imls.gov/)

Trends in Funding and Prospecting

Trends vary according to the source of funding: whether from a parent organization as part of the budgeting process or from corporate, foundation, government, or individual sources. Common to all are certain themes. Funding bodies respond favorably to projects that focus on the audience; address demographics; are built on collaborations; link or engage state, local, regional networks; demonstrate innovation or leadership; and build on the library as cultural center.

Focus on the Audience. Funding bodies do not always want to hear "the library needs . . ." but rather "the community will benefit. . . ." In seeking funds, focus on the ultimate benefits and outcomes and how they correspond with the funder's objectives.

Address Demographics. Target your audience. Match your audience to prospective funders' interests in their target audiences. Focus on the unique nature of library audiences.

Build on Collaborations. Collaboration helps prospective funders see that you have other support in your community, and it shows involvement of potential and intended audiences.

Link or Engage State, Local, Regional Networks. Engaging, creating, or connecting with existing networks can build a learning environment and foster efficiency. Like collaborations, networks offer opportunities to make connections and to be effective and flexible at the grassroots level, which can be appealing to funders.

Demonstrate Innovation or Leadership. Be the first institution in your community to take the lead in an area or issue; cast your community's struggle in a different light; build a bridge; reach out to an underserved group; leverage a new activity or new participation.

Build on the Library as Cultural Center. The library is an existing organization in which funders can reliably invest. Libraries are capable of community building and have the inherent resources to offer longer-term opportunities. From the funder's perspective, the library has a unique role and niche, demonstrated by the following traits:

- Hub of community
- Sense of place
- Lifelong learning
- Unique ability to serve all
- Neutrality
- Democratic setting
- Appropriate spaces created by library building boom
- Growth of adult programming resulting in increased community expectations
- High percentage of cardholders among diverse populations

Information on Trends and Prospecting

Fund-raising is an industry unto itself. Websites and print titles on the subject abound. The following are just a few resources for librarians interested in trends and prospects in arts and cultural funding as well as funding in general:

Chronicle of Philanthropy, print and online
(http://philanthropy.com/)

Arts and Culture Funding Report
(http://www.capitolcitypublishers.com/pubs/arts/)

Foundation Center research
(http://fdncenter.org/research/trends_analysis/)

American Association of Fundraising Counsel—*Giving USA* report, available to members only
(http://www.aafrc.org/)

Philanthropy Journal
(http://www.philanthropyjournal.org/front.asp/)

Cultural Policy and the Arts National Data Archive
(http://www.cpanda.org/)

Proposal Writing

Communicating your ideas on paper in response to opportunities is a central part of fund-raising. To have the best shot at success in an application process or a competition for proposals, take the time to adhere to all requirements and to present your information compellingly. The suggestions in box 7-1 are adapted from "Writing Grant Applications: Some

BOX 7-1

RESPONDING TO REQUESTS FOR PROPOSALS: MAKING YOUR APPLICATION COMPETITIVE

1. Applications that are thorough and organized stand out to reviewers. Spend time writing the proposal, thinking of ideas for programs, and lining up support in the library and in the community, and you will see better results in both the application process and when developing and implementing the program.

2. Read the application guidelines carefully and answer all questions directly and with as much detail as possible. Pay particular attention to requirements mentioned in the application. For example, ALA's *Jazz Age in Paris* traveling exhibition application stipulated that programs consisting only of musical performances were not considered humanities programs as defined by the program funder. Therefore, libraries that submitted applications that offered only musical performances as the required humanities program did not receive grants.

3. Think beyond the boundaries of normal library operating procedures in completing your application. If your application states that you plan to publicize a program through all of the normal channels, rely on an audience that already attends programs, or focus on standard program formats, it will not compare favorably with an application that offers new publicity strategies to attract new audiences, presents creative ideas for programs, and demonstrates that the library will approach the project with a fresh outlook in order to make it a success.

4. Submit letters of support from collaborating groups you mention in your application and plan to work with on the project. Their presence adds weight to your application and shows that you are committed to making the program succeed.

5. If you use statistics to describe your service area, your targeted audience, or any other part of the proposal, be sure you indicate how or where they were obtained, or use reasonable estimates and indicate their basis.

6. Think through the answer to each question on the application. Be careful not to restate a question, and make sure that each answer provides detail and shows your commitment to the program.

7. Provide all signatures and attachments requested. For example, if a scholar is required for a project, you must submit the scholar's résumé with your application, or the application will be considered incomplete.

8. Pay close attention to your application's appearance, clarity, enthusiasm, spelling, and organization. Ask yourself: if I were the reviewer, what would be my impression of this proposal? Would I find it easy to follow and understand? Would I be excited by the programs proposed? Use boldface type, bullets, italics, and other devices to make points and help organize your proposal, but be careful not to overdo it. Use simple, direct sentences. Check and double-check spelling. Convey your own excitement about the project.

9. Read the original application guidelines carefully after you have completed your proposal to be sure that you have answered all questions, are submitting the attachments required, have all signatures, and have met other requirements.

Susan Brandehoff, American Library Association Public Programs Office

Helpful Hints," which is intended for applicants seeking ALA Public Programs Office projects and can be found at http://www.ala.org/ala/ppo/grantsandevents/writinggrantapps/writinggrant.htm/.

Relationships and Networks

A well-known adage in the fund-raising world is that people give to people. As in any other aspect of life, relationships are important. On occasion, a great idea and a letter-perfect proposal may be all you need. But in the long run, you must be consistent in cultivating and maintaining relationships with funders and develop a stellar record of delivering on your promises to provide well-run programs that make a difference.

Meeting and networking with potential funders, grantors, and donors can be facilitated by getting to know and becoming known by your patrons, be they local business owners, arts and humanities administrators, philanthropy-minded individuals, or simply library fans. Go beyond the gathering of program evaluations and mingle with your audiences before and after the programs. Audiences will often express their reactions, opinions, and feelings out loud rather than put them in writing. By the same token it is invaluable when seeking feedback, funding, and general support to make sure that people associate a caring and competent person with any query, appeal, or request.

Maintaining fruitful relationships is at least as important as cultivating new ones—and may be even more important. Both new and established providers of funds are interested in how easy you are to work with, whether you can effectively produce what you propose, and whether the work you do with the resources they provide will have the desired outcome. They want you to succeed so that they in turn will succeed.

Think of grant writing—writing proposals or completing applications in response to requests for proposals—as the tip of the iceberg. To be successful, you will need to research the priorities of funding bodies, meet people and cultivate relationships, and maintain positive ongoing working relationships. Be patient and persistent. Be gracious and thoughtful. Be reliable. Address problems directly when they arise. Take opportunities to report progress and to say thank you.

CHAPTER 8

Marketing and Public Relations for Programming

Every library should try to be complete on something, if it were only the history of pinheads. —OLIVER WENDELL HOLMES SR.

King County Library System Issaquah, Washington

Visibility for and public awareness about the library and its services are important reasons for presenting cultural programming. Although the primary aim in marketing programming is to encourage the library's target audience to attend, the benefit of good public relations (PR) will far exceed the attendance count for any single event. Many people who do not attend will want to know what the library is doing and will appreciate your publicity efforts.

To draw the desired audience and create awareness about a programming series, a library needs to plan and implement an effective promotional campaign. The guidelines and examples in this chapter are intended to help in launching a successful campaign. Remember: to ensure ongoing goodwill and support, it is essential to acknowledge sponsors, funders, and collaborating organizations in all promotional materials.

Getting Started

To meet media and other deadlines, start promoting the series at least two months in advance (see the planning calendar, figure 2-4, in chapter 2). First, determine your target audience (chapters 2 and 3), your goals for audience size, and the best communication methods for your series. Involve fellow staff members in program planning and foster new ideas and additional support and enthusiasm. During a brainstorming session,

> emphasize the potential for recruiting new users and building support for the library;
>
> communicate the goals for the program—target audiences and desired outcomes;
>
> assign staff with various interests/talents to work in small groups to carry out the goals.

Share programming plans with the library director, the board, Friends, and other library support groups, and invite their ideas and cooperation.

Defining the Target Audience

General promotional materials, such as flyers, press releases, and advertisements, are great vehicles for reaching a general audience of mixed ages and backgrounds. However, there are probably several groups in the community that will be particularly interested in the series. These groups can provide support by passing information on to members who may be interested in attending or providing financial and other support. The following types of community organizations may be interested in the library's cultural programming events, depending on the topics:

- Local historical societies and groups
- Book clubs
- Writers' groups
- Museums, galleries, and art councils
- Chambers of Commerce
- VFW chapters

- American Legion groups
- Minority group associations
- Labor unions
- Kiwanis and Rotary clubs
- Local college and university groups or classes
- Local high-school classes
- Local elementary- and high-school teachers, college and university professors and staff
- Professional associations and societies
- Councils on aging
- Senior centers
- AARP groups
- Lifelong learning societies and educational centers

Also, depending on the topic of your series, there may be other organizations with a particular interest in your program. For example, a library hosting a film series focused on aspects of twentieth-century technologies might target filmmaking groups, electronic communications and filmmaking classes, technology company employee groups and unions, and engineering and technology centers.

Choosing Your Communication Methods

Once you have determined who you would like to participate in the programming, you can focus on how to let them know about the event. Most communication methods fall into four categories:

Public Relations/Publicity. Newspaper and magazine articles, announcements on television and radio programs, websites, web publicity, public service announcements (PSAs), letters to the editor

Direct Marketing. Direct mailings, mass e-mail messages, web marketing

Personal Contact. Word of mouth, public speaking engagements, telephone, e-mails, letters

Advertising. Print ads, TV and radio spots, banners, flyers, bookmarks, posters, buttons, displays

Public Relations and Publicity

The keys to getting your message out to a mass audience are contacting the media and using the Web. Send a *press release* announcing the event to local newspapers, radio stations, and television stations at least two to four weeks before the event. (See figure 8-1 for a sample press release.) If there are regional magazines or talk shows that promote upcoming events, send a release to them as well. Because magazines often have longer lead times, send their press releases out at least four to eight weeks before the event.

FIGURE 8-1   Sample News Release Announcing Library Exhibition

THE LIBRARY
OF VIRGINIA

PRESS RELEASE

Elizabeth I: Ruler and Legend To Run Through February 18 at The Library of Virginia

Contact: Janice M. Hathcock   For Immediate Release
            604/692-3592
            jhathcock@lva.lib.va.us

   (Richmond, Va.) -- Opening on December 22, 2003, and continuing through February 18, 2004, *Elizabeth I: Ruler and Legend* will be on view in the Library of Virginia's exhibition gallery. Organized by the Center for Renaissance Studies at Chicago's Newberry Library, in collaboration with the American Library Association, this exhibition explores Elizabeth's patronage of the arts, her interest in exploring and building England into a world power, the court intrigues that threatened to dethrone her and the reasons she never married. The exhibition uses images reproduced from rare books, manuscripts, maps, letters, paintings and artifacts from the Newberry Library and other institutions. *Elizabeth I: Ruler and Legend* is a national traveling exhibition organized by the Newberry Library's Center for Renaissance Studies in collaboration with the American Library Association Public Programs Office. It is based on a major exhibition of the same name mounted by the Newberry Library in 2003 to commemorate the reign of Queen Elizabeth I on the 400th anniversary of her death. The Newberry Library is an independent humanities research library, and is free and open to the public. This exhibition has been made possible in part by two major grants from the National Endowment for the Humanities for promoting excellence in the humanities. Major support for the exhibition is also provided by the Vance Family Fund and the University of Illinois at Chicago.

   The Library of Virginia is located in historic downtown Richmond at 800 East Broad Street. The exhibition is **free** and open to the public Monday through Saturday from 9:00 a.m. until 5:00 p.m. The reading rooms and collections are open to the public Tuesday through Saturday. There is free parking for Library visitors in the Library's underground deck accessible from either 8th or 9th streets. For information on free, complementary programs associated with the exhibition please visit our Web site at www.lva.lib.va.us.

#

December 5, 2003

800 East Broad Street • Richmond, VA 23219-8000 • (804) 692-3592

If possible, address press releases to a specific reporter. Call local media outlets to confirm deadlines and submission requirements and to find out who covers community, arts, or literary events. Send releases to that person's attention. If a specific name is not available, address press releases to the news desk for larger publications or to the editor for smaller publications. Most media outlets prefer to receive press releases via fax, but it is acceptable to use the mail when sending additional materials, such as a brochure or a bookmark advertising the event, with the release. If any of the publications you are contacting also prints a calendar of events, be sure to send a press release to the contact for that section. Quite often, publications will run articles about upcoming events and include related information in their community calendar sections.

About a week before your event, follow up the press release by faxing a *media alert* to key contacts. As illustrated in figure 8-2, the alert provides

FIGURE 8-2   Sample Media Letter Sent to Media List

October 18, 2003

Decatur Public Library is pleased to announce the opening of a thought-provoking new exhibit, *Forever Free: Abraham Lincoln's Journey to Emancipation,* on November 17, 2003. The library was selected as one of only 39 libraries in the United States, and the first in Illinois, to host the traveling exhibition. *Forever Free* was organized by The Huntington Library, San Marino, Calif., and the Gilder Lehrman Institute of American History, New York City, in cooperation with the American Library Association Public Programs Office.

Forever Free is made possible by a major grant from the National Endowment for the Humanities. It is based on original documents about Abraham Lincoln, the Civil War, abolition, and the Emancipation Proclamation in the collections of the Huntington Library and the Gilder Lehrman Institute of American History.

We would like to invite you to attend the opening ceremony for the exhibit on Monday, November 17, 2003, at 10:00 a.m. The enclosed media kit provides additional details about *Forever Free* and the variety of programs we have scheduled in conjunction with the exhibit. I would ask that you not publish this information until at least 2 weeks prior to the opening.

I would be happy to speak to you further about these exciting events. Please contact me at 217-421-9771 or by e-mail at sdpointon@decatur.lib.il.us for additional details.

We hope you will join us as we introduce this fascinating exhibit to the community.

Sincerely,

Sandra D. Pointon
Head of Adult Division

Decatur Public Library, Decatur, Illinois

specific information about the date, time, and location for reporters and photographers who may be interested in attending the event or including the information in a column about upcoming events. If possible, call contacts a day or two later to confirm that they received the media alert, to find out if they have any questions, and to see if they are interested in attending or getting more information about the program.

For media professionals who are interested in attending the event or in getting more information, have additional materials available in a *press kit*. The press kit should contain one copy of the press release and the media alert, photos and biographies of presenters and other key participants, and copies of all promotional materials—flyers, bookmarks, buttons, and the like. If there is an opportunity to discuss the event with a reporter, suggest story ideas and offer to schedule an interview with the presenter (after making sure that the presenter is willing to be interviewed).

Since television and radio stations are required to use a percentage of their airtime for not-for-profit and public announcements, local stations may be willing to air a *public service announcement* about the library programming. A PSA will advertise the event, but the airtime is donated, so there is no cost to the library. Some sample PSAs are presented in figure 8-3.

Using the *Web* to promote events is very important. If the library's website does not have a "Coming Events" section, talk to the webmaster about creating one. It is the ideal place for library patrons to find out details about programming series. Include as much information as possible on the website. (See figure 8-4 for a sample web promotion from the Boulder [Colo.] Public Library.) Although some current library patrons may use the website to find other information or to learn about upcoming events, very few new or potential patrons are likely to visit the site without prompting. The Web is a key way to provide information to patrons and community members who may have heard about an event through other means but need details about the date, time, location, topics discussed, and so forth.

If you post information about the series on the library's website, include the web address on all promotional materials. Using just your library's short address (such as www.ala.org) is acceptable and usually easier to read. Although some promotional materials still carry long addresses (http://www.ala.org/), they are not necessary since most browsers are configured to automatically place http:// before an address. However, if your library has an address with a different hyper tag, such as https://, include it in the address.

Other organizations' websites can be useful for getting the word out about library events. Of course you will want to include links from your site to the sites of your collaborating organizations. In addition, city governments, community centers, local media outlets, and Chambers of Commerce may post information about community events on their websites. Many major cities also have web-based entertainment and event guides, like citysearch.com, which provides information about events in several cities. If such websites exist in the area, contact their staffs about posting library events and information. Many of these sites will post information about not-for-profit organizations' events free of charge.

FIGURE 8-3   Sample Public Service Announcement Copy

For Immediate Release
Contact: Jenifer Baldwin, W. W. Hagerty Library, Drexel University
frankenstein@drexel.edu
215.895.2772
www.library.drexel.edu/frankenstein/

Public Service Announcements

:15   For nearly two centuries, the story of Frankenstein has gripped our imaginations and haunted our nightmares. Come to Drexel University's W. W. Hagerty Library, 33rd & Market Streets, Philadelphia, to see an exciting new traveling exhibition about Mary Shelley's fascinating book. It runs from February 7, 2003, through March 21, 2003.

For more information about the library's schedule of programs for the exhibition, please visit www.library.drexel.edu/frankenstein/ or call 215.895.2772.

:20   Everyone knows the story of Frankenstein. Or do they? The tale of the ambitious scientist and the monster he creates is now nearly two hundred years old. A new traveling exhibition at Drexel University's W. W. Hagerty Library offers a fresh look at Mary Shelley's book and its importance in discussions about social responsibility. It also shows Boris Karloff as the monster and features colorful posters from Frankenstein movies. Come to Drexel University's W. W. Hagerty Library, 33rd & Market Streets, Philadelphia from February 7, 2003, through March 21, 2003, to see for yourself what Frankenstein is all about.

For more information about the library's schedule of programs for the exhibition, please visit www.library.drexel.edu/frankenstein/ or call 215.895.2772.

:30   Most people think they know the story of Frankenstein. But did you realize that Mary Shelley imagined her monster as a sensitive, well-read creature who craved human companionship, not the speechless killer we see in the movies? And Frankenstein is not the <u>monster's</u> name.

Drexel University's W. W. Hagerty Library invites you to explore the fascinating story of the ambitious scientist Victor Frankenstein and the monster he creates in his lab at a free exhibition called "Frankenstein: Penetrating the Secrets of Nature." The exhibition offers a fresh look at Mary Shelley's book and its importance in discussions about social responsibility and ethical scientific research. It also shows Boris Karloff as the monster and features colorful posters from Frankenstein movies. It will be on display from February 7, 2003, through March 21, 2003. Exciting free public lectures and film series will also be offered throughout the six weeks of the exhibition.

The Frankenstein exhibition was organized by the National Library of Medicine and the American Library Association with grants from the National Endowment for the Humanities and the National Library of Medicine. Additional support for local programs and events has been provided by the Pennsylvania Humanities Council and the Francis C. Wood Institute for the History of Medicine of the College of Physicians of Philadelphia.

For more information about the library's schedule of programs for the exhibition, please visit www.library.drexel.edu/frankenstein/ or call 215.895.2772.

'Frankenstein: Penetrating the Secrets of Nature"
Drexel University Libraries
www.library.drexel.edu/frankenstein/
frankenstein@drexel.edu
215.895.2772

W. W. Hagerty Library, Drexel University

FIGURE 8-4   Sample Website Page Promoting Program

Used with permission of the Boulder Public Library, Boulder, Colorado

Direct Marketing

Use direct marketing to contact target organizations and individual group members. When contacting community and other organizations, use a personalized letter or phone call. A copy of the program flyer can be used as an informal letter, if needed, but include a personal note, especially if you are asking for financial or other support. Also send an e-mail message about the program to community group leaders to post to their electronic discussion groups or forward to their own address lists.

In addition to contacting organizations and their members, target individuals in your community. If the library keeps a list of patrons' e-mail addresses, sending a mass e-mail message about the upcoming event can be an effective and inexpensive way to get the word out to a number of people. If e-mail addresses are not available, consider creating a postcard to mail to library patrons, community members, or others. See figure 8-5 for an example.

Personal Contact

Personal contact can be one of the most effective means of communicating with key individuals and groups. It can create better understanding and generate more enthusiasm than any other communication method.

Create a list of influential individuals in your community—the mayor, city council members, business leaders, and the like—who may be interested in the series. Send a letter and program flyer about the event and ask to meet with them for further discussion. If a meeting is not possible, call within a week to follow up. Even if influential individuals are not able to participate in the series, letting them know about the program could help the library in other ways.

When contacting community groups, ask to speak for five to ten minutes at one of their upcoming meetings or events. At the meeting, outline the overall series plan and present convincing reasons why the series may be of interest to group members. Bring flyers, bookmarks, and other materials to hand out. If possible, speak at the end of the meeting or offer to stay until the end of the meeting to answer questions.

If speaking at meetings is not possible, ask group leaders to pass out flyers or mention the program to their members and staff. Figure 8-6 provides a sample cover letter that you can adapt and send to community groups along with your promotional materials.

Advertising

Although advertising can be expensive, it can also be one of the most effective ways of promoting your program. Among the most common methods of advertising are promotional flyers and posters, paid ads, and bookmarks, buttons, and other promotional items.

Promotional flyers and posters should be simple and include the basic title or theme for the series, an identifying graphic; the titles of individual events as well as their times, places, presenters' names, and brief biographical information; acknowledgment of funders and program partners; and, if applicable, the library's web address. Flyers and posters can be displayed at the library, community centers (such as city hall, the post office,

FIGURE 8-5 Sample Library Program Postcard Announcement

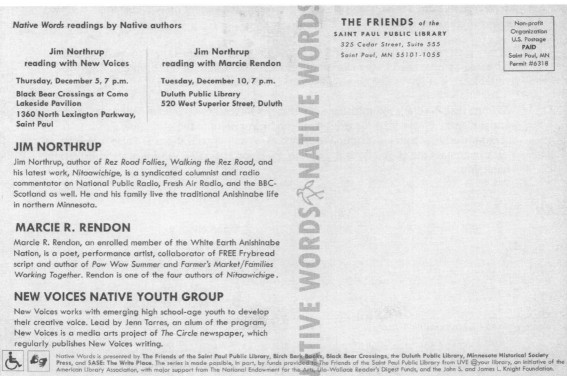

Native Words readings by Native authors

Jim Northrup
reading with New Voices

Thursday, December 5, 7 p.m.

Black Bear Crossings at Como Lakeside Pavilion
1360 North Lexington Parkway, Saint Paul

Jim Northrup
reading with Marcie Rendon

Tuesday, December 10, 7 p.m.

Duluth Public Library
520 West Superior Street, Duluth

JIM NORTHRUP

Jim Northrup, author of *Rez Road Follies, Walking the Rez Road,* and his latest work, *Nitaawichige,* is a syndicated columnist and radio commentator on National Public Radio, Fresh Air Radio, and the BBC-Scotland as well. He and his family live the traditional Anishinabe life in northern Minnesota.

MARCIE R. RENDON

Marcie R. Rendon, an enrolled member of the White Earth Anishinabe Nation, is a poet, performance artist, collaborator of FREE Frybread script and author of *Pow Wow Summer* and *Farmer's Market/Families Working Together.* Rendon is one of the four authors of *Nitaawichige*.

NEW VOICES NATIVE YOUTH GROUP

New Voices works with emerging high school-age youth to develop their creative voice. Lead by Jenn Torres, an alum of the program, New Voices is a media arts project of *The Circle* newspaper, which regularly publishes New Voices writing.

THE FRIENDS of the
SAINT PAUL PUBLIC LIBRARY
325 Cedar Street, Suite 555
Saint Paul, MN 55101-1055

Non-profit
Organization
U.S. Postage
PAID
Saint Paul, MN
Permit #6318

Native Words is presented by **The Friends of the Saint Paul Public Library, Birch Bark Books, Black Bear Crossings, the Duluth Public Library, Minnesota Historical Society Press,** and **SASE: The Write Place.** The series is made possible, in part, by funds provided to The Friends of the Saint Paul Public Library from LIVE @your library, an initiative of the American Library Association, with major support from The National Endowment for the Arts, Lila-Wallace Reader's Digest Funds, and the John S. and James L. Knight Foundation.

The Friends of the Saint Paul Library, Saint Paul, Minnesota

FIGURE 8-6   Sample Letter to Community Group

SAINT LOUIS PUBLIC LIBRARY

October 17, 2003

Dear Sir or Madam:

From November 12 through January 9, St. Louis Public Library will have on display the national traveling exhibition, **Frankenstein: Penetrating the Secrets of Nature**. This exhibition examines the monster and the scientist whose story has become one of the most enduring myths of the Western world since Mary Shelley published her book, *Frankenstein*, in 1818. It also illustrates how Frankenstein has become a symbol for public fears about groundbreaking new scientific techniques which often challenge our understanding of what is "natural" such as cloning, organ transplants, or genetically modified foods.

The exhibit arrives after Veterans Day and runs through Friday, January 9, 2004. It will be available to view at Central Library in the Great Hall, Second Floor. Central Library is located at 1301 Olive Street and the hours are noted in the enclosed brochure. The exhibit will be available to view all the hours the Library is open. Please also note the Frankenstein Film Series, the opening reception for the exhibit on November 17, and two other programs scheduled.

Library staff have compiled a select bibliography to complement the variety of issues addressed by or related to the exhibit. Because of the length of this bibliography, it is available only at www.slpl.lib.mo.us which is the Library's web site.

We hope that the enclosed information will be of interest to you, your colleagues, and your students. Please visit the exhibit, attend one or more of the programs, and encourage others to do so. Group visits by classes and organizations are also welcome. You can contact me at bmcdonald@slpl.lib.mo.us or 314-539-0348 for more information. Thank you.

Sincerely,

Brenda McDonald
Director of Central Services

schools, and local colleges), restaurants, grocery stores, dry cleaners, bookstores, health clubs, and other public places. Ask Friends and trustees to put up flyers and posters at their local merchants' shops. See figure 8-7 for a sample flyer.

FIGURE 8-7   Sample Flyer for Use by Local Merchants

Design by Maggie Bice, Graphic Designer, Central Rappahannock Regional Library, Fredericksburg, Virginia

Paid advertising in local newspapers and on local radio or television stations, although effective, can be especially costly. Before considering paid advertising, approach your local newspapers and radio and television stations regarding public service announcements (as discussed previously under "Public Relations and Publicity"). Some newspapers and broadcast stations may be willing to donate or discount airtime or ad space for not-for-profit groups. Acknowledge media outlets as sponsors on program materials if they provide free advertising. If you decide to use paid advertising, look to the library's Friends or other groups to underwrite costs. The Cuyahoga County (Ohio) Public Library placed the ad shown in figure 8-8 in both the *Plain Dealer* newspaper and *Cleveland* magazine. Note that the library acknowledges many sources of funding and support in the ad.

Develop simple, cost-effective *bookmarks*, *buttons*, or other promotional items to promote series events. Such items can double as freebies for patrons who attend the series. Hand out promotional items at schools, community group meetings, and other locations and events. Ask Friends and trustees to hand out bookmarks to friends and colleagues. The Kansas City Public Library developed the effective brochure and bookmark shown in figures 8-9 and 8-10 to promote their program Frankenstein: Penetrating the Secrets of Nature.

Putting It All Together

Spend a little time thinking about which marketing and public relations methods will work best for your program series, community, and library. Consider the budget and the time available. Reflect on the planning team—will the event be produced by one person or by a committee? And take into account past successes and failures by evaluating which communication methods worked best to promote previous events. Combine some successful methods used before with some new ideas.

Keep in mind goals for the size and type of audience the series will attract. If the library can hold only fifty people, do not spend hundreds of dollars on publicity. Instead, use resources wisely. Focus on contacting the individuals and groups who will be most interested instead of trying to reach everybody in town. It is important to make sure that the public is aware of library events, but you can usually accomplish that simply with flyers and a few press releases to key media outlets, and you can spend the remaining time on contacting people by letter and phone.

In contrast, if the goal is to attract a group of two hundred people who have never set foot in the library, your promotional activities will need to be more creative. Spending extra time and effort on contacting new people and developing promotional materials for new outlets and locations could have a substantial payoff. When a program brings new faces into the library, it invariably results in the issuing of more library cards and the enthusiasm of new, lifelong library patrons.

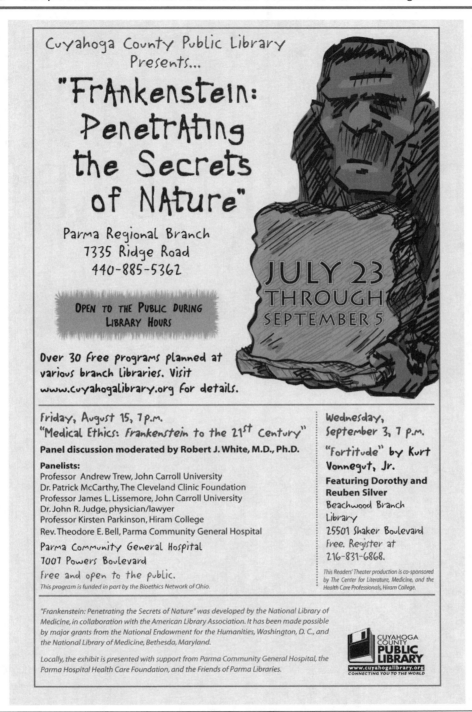

Cuyahoga County Public Library, Parma, Ohio

FIGURE 8-9   Sample Brochure Panel

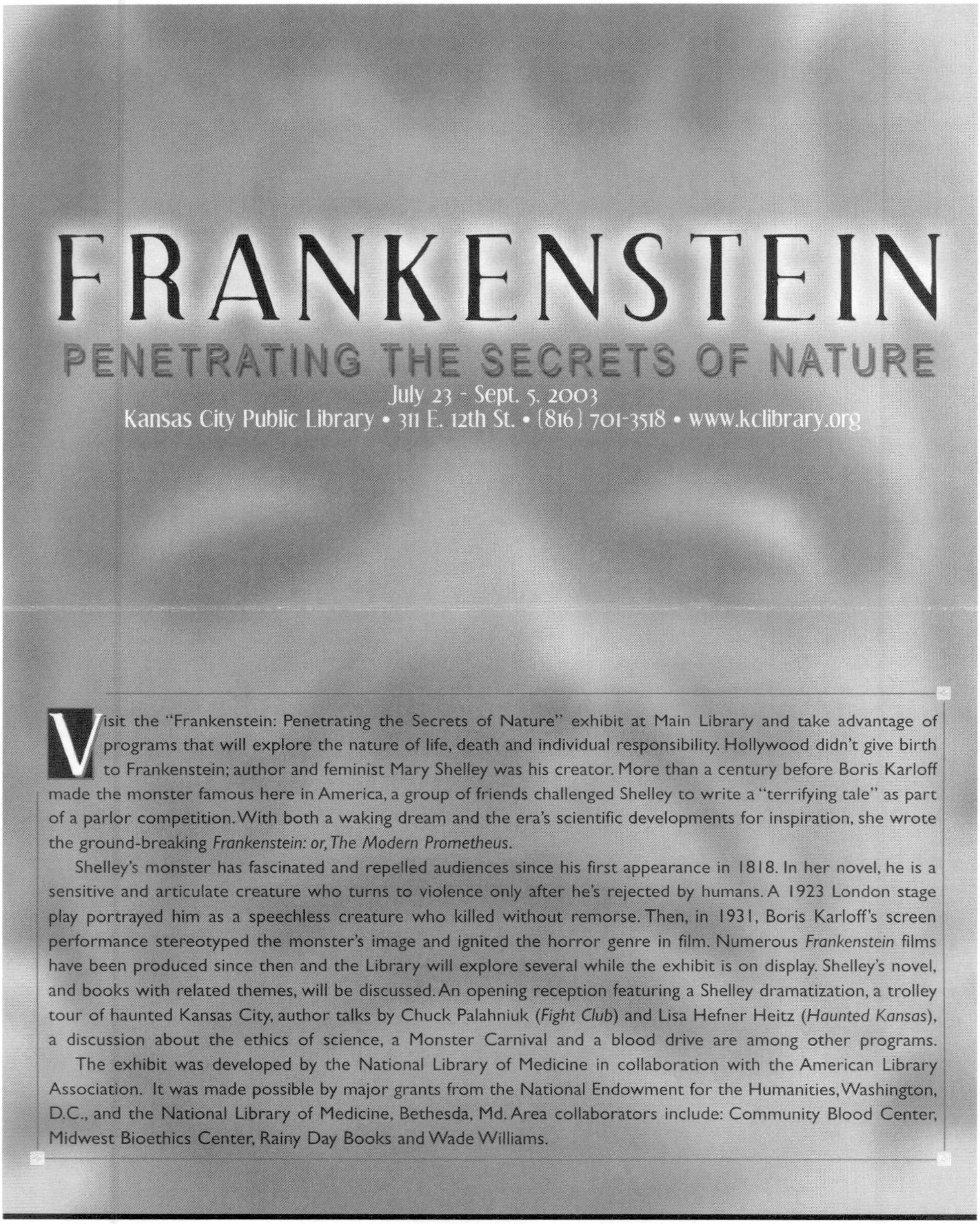

FRANKENSTEIN
PENETRATING THE SECRETS OF NATURE
July 23 - Sept. 5, 2003
Kansas City Public Library • 311 E. 12th St. • (816) 701-3518 • www.kclibrary.org

Visit the "Frankenstein: Penetrating the Secrets of Nature" exhibit at Main Library and take advantage of programs that will explore the nature of life, death and individual responsibility. Hollywood didn't give birth to Frankenstein; author and feminist Mary Shelley was his creator. More than a century before Boris Karloff made the monster famous here in America, a group of friends challenged Shelley to write a "terrifying tale" as part of a parlor competition. With both a waking dream and the era's scientific developments for inspiration, she wrote the ground-breaking *Frankenstein: or, The Modern Prometheus.*

Shelley's monster has fascinated and repelled audiences since his first appearance in 1818. In her novel, he is a sensitive and articulate creature who turns to violence only after he's rejected by humans. A 1923 London stage play portrayed him as a speechless creature who killed without remorse. Then, in 1931, Boris Karloff's screen performance stereotyped the monster's image and ignited the horror genre in film. Numerous *Frankenstein* films have been produced since then and the Library will explore several while the exhibit is on display. Shelley's novel, and books with related themes, will be discussed. An opening reception featuring a Shelley dramatization, a trolley tour of haunted Kansas City, author talks by Chuck Palahniuk (*Fight Club*) and Lisa Hefner Heitz (*Haunted Kansas*), a discussion about the ethics of science, a Monster Carnival and a blood drive are among other programs.

The exhibit was developed by the National Library of Medicine in collaboration with the American Library Association. It was made possible by major grants from the National Endowment for the Humanities, Washington, D.C., and the National Library of Medicine, Bethesda, Md. Area collaborators include: Community Blood Center, Midwest Bioethics Center, Rainy Day Books and Wade Williams.

The Kansas City Public Library Marketing Department, Kansas City, Missouri

FIGURE 8-10   Sample Bookmark

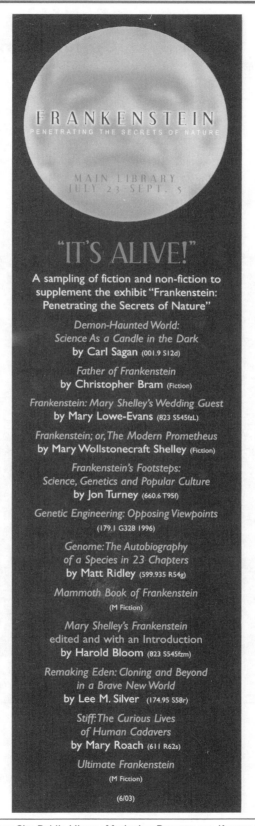

The Kansas City Public Library Marketing Department, Kansas City, Missouri

Conclusion

The library is our house of intellect,
our transcendental university, with
one exception: no one graduates
from a library. No one possibly can,
and no one should.

—VARTAN GREGORIAN

Courtesy of the Omaha Public Library

No book can provide everything the programmer needs. Whether you are a beginning programmer or an expert, being successful over the long run requires continuous networking, learning, and interacting with peers and colleagues. And to stay fresh and engaged, you will need to seek ideas, inspiration, advice, training, and turnkey programs from a multitude of sources.

Few libraries have positions dedicated solely to adult programming. Typically adult programming duties are combined with a variety of other responsibilities, including, but not limited to, children's and youth programming, reference and reader's advisory, public relations, and development.

For many staff this translates into long hours and the need to fit programming in around the "real" work. It is important that staff undertaking such a difficult task and working such long hours feel compensated by personal interest in the program content and gratified by the quality of the programming and the engagement of audiences.

It is also important to have the support and cooperation of administration and colleagues. This is gained by engaging other staff in planning and implementation and by consistently communicating about what will happen and what did happen.

Engage volunteers as well as colleagues in the work. Collaborate with other community organizations. Involve their members in program planning and implementation. Network with colleagues in the field to stay inspired.

Remember, success breeds success. Among the factors that contribute to programming success:

- The administration supports programming activities.
- The entire staff knows about the programming.
- The programmer enjoys a sense of experimentation: it takes time and trial and error to build audiences.
- Themes are used to develop and promote programming.
- The goals of programming are clearly defined.
- The programmer is aware of the other activities taking place in the community.
- The library has realistic expectations about audience sizes for various activities.

Networking and staying involved with colleagues and opportunities for continuing education will make your job easier. Sign up for electronic discussion lists such as Publib, PRTalk, and the ALA Public Programs Office list; cruise websites such as the ALA Public Programs Office Cultural Programming Online Resource Center (http://www.ala.org/publicprograms/orc/); attend conferences and workshops as well as book, arts, and humanities festivals; read the professional literature—and publish!

Enjoy the work of bringing ideas to life and creating cultural programming that truly makes a difference in your community and in people's lives.

Five Star Program Series

Excellence in cultural programming can be achieved by presenting a coherent thematic series of programs that are compelling to a community's audience, help build a diverse audience over time, and feature appropriately qualified presenters. The ten programs profiled in this section, which come from libraries of various sizes and types, met those criteria.

Other factors that contributed to the programs' excellence were strong local partnerships that enhanced the programming, the acquisition of adequate financial resources, the employment of effective marketing and outreach strategies, the achievement of desired or projected attendance figures, and the triumph of making a difference in the community. We present these examples of excellence with the hope that they will inspire other programmers to raise the bar for programming in their own libraries.

Chicano and Latino Writers Festival 2003
(Seventh Annual)

The Friends of the Saint Paul (Minn.) Public Library

COLLABORATING ORGANIZATIONS

Adams Spanish Immersion School, Guadalupe Alternative Programs, Metropolitan State University, the Minnesota Twins, Neighborhood House, Ruminator Books, and the Creative Writing Program at the University of Minnesota and the Edelstein-Keller Endowment for Visiting Writers.

SIZE OF LIBRARY SERVICE AREA

287,151 (metro region: 3 million)

DESCRIPTION OF PROGRAMS

The Chicano and Latino Writers Festival features local and national writers. Featured authors in past years have included Isabel Allende, Esmeralda Santiago, Luis Rodriguez, and Juan Felipe Herrera, as well as nationally recognized Minnesota writers such as Ray Gonzalez, Sandra Benitez, and George Rabasa. The festival also includes a program with high-school writers and a Days of the Dead event. The festival usually runs from the early October to mid-November and is based at the Riverview Branch Library.

FORMAT AND PRESENTERS

Chillin' with Salsa—part reading, part performance, partially bilingual with some children's work—Juan Felipe Herrera, writer and scholar, author of nineteen books for children and adults, from poetry to short stories to prose and picture books.

Diario en Medellín—documentary film.

Reading from recent works and work in progress—Diego Vázquez Jr., novelist and poetry slam icon.

Reading and reception—Luis Alberto Urrea.

Días de muertos—display of traditional and innovative *ofrendas*, poetry, stories, and music to celebrate Mexico's Days of the Dead tradition.

Home Is Everything: The Latino Baseball Story—presented by author Marcos Bretón and photographer José Luis Villegas, along with local hero Tony Oliva.

The Movies of My Life/Las peliculas de mi vida—presentation by Chilean author, editor, and journalist Alberto Fuguet.

Our Voice—bilingual presentation by students and mentors about intergenerational experiences and cultural tensions.

LOCATION OF PROGRAMS

Riverview Branch Library (5), Guadalupe Alternative Programs (1), Metropolitan State University Auditorium (1), Ruminator Books (1).

TARGET AUDIENCE

The primary target audience was the Chicano/Latino community in Saint Paul. The secondary target audience was the broader community interested in literature and Chicano/Latino culture.

ATTENDANCE

Approximately 1,000, including about 30 percent Chicano or Latino. (About 10 percent of Saint Paul's population is Chicano/Latino.)

MARKETING AND PUBLICITY METHODS

Special brochure/mailing, feature in calendar/newsletter, flyers in library branches, press releases to 100+ media outlets metrowide, with special focus on Latino and neighborhood newspapers.

BUDGET

$22,000; includes $13,000 in grant funding, in-kind costs (not including staff time), and approximately $4,000 of Friends' own programming funds.

Old Sounds in New Lands:
A Celebration of Kentucky's Appalachian Music

Eastern Kentucky University Libraries

COLLABORATING ORGANIZATIONS

None.

SIZE OF LIBRARY SERVICE AREA

566,768

DESCRIPTION OF PROGRAMS

Series of public programs on the evolution of Kentucky's Appalachian music.

FORMAT AND PRESENTERS

Lecture, performance, and reception: Transplanted Roots: Anglo-Celtic Origins, featuring speakers and performers Pale, Stout, and Amber.

Lecture, performance, and reception: Mountain Soil: Ingredients for a New Sound, featuring Dr. Ron Pen and folksinger Jean Ritchie.

Lecture, performance, and reception: Bluegrass Branch: Pickin' Up the Tempo, featuring dulcimer maker Homer Ledford with the Cabin Creek Band.

Related film series presented the week of each lecture.

LOCATION OF PROGRAMS

Lectures and receptions: University Library

Performances: University Theater

TARGET AUDIENCE

People of immediate region, beyond university community, with interest in Appalachian music; kindergarten through grade 12 music and social studies teachers and students; university community.

ATTENDANCE

Transplanted Roots: Anglo-Celtic Origins: 250

Jean Ritchie: 470

Homer Ledford with the Cabin Creek Band: 530

MARKETING AND PUBLICITY METHODS

Series poster distributed throughout region in schools, stores, music shops, and banks; campus radio promotion; area radio PSAs; pitching to area daily arts critic; electronic list e-mail announcements, including a sound file, to music teachers and district school offices.

BUDGET

$5,750 ($2,100 LIVE! grant)

Portals of Change

Greenwich (Conn.) Library, Greenwich

COLLABORATING ORGANIZATIONS

Urban Artists Initiative, Institute for Community Research, United Way of Greenwich, Clementine Lockwood Peterson Foundation, Greenwich Library Board of Trustees.

SIZE OF LIBRARY SERVICE AREA

61,101

DESCRIPTION OF PROGRAMS

October 6–7, 2001: Two-day theme-based cultural symposium for family, youth, and adult library audiences to explore tradition and ideas of change within our community at large through music, myth, dance, poetry, and architecture.

FORMAT AND PRESENTERS

Sculptural display of portals and castles by Shaw Stuart as focus for theme. Participants invited to physically move through the piece as an introduction to each segment of the program. Morning and afternoon sessions, introduced and completed with discussions led by presenters, included storytelling, art discussion by children, computer graphics and web design, poets in action, dance conversations, Indian classical dance, concert of Peruvian music, and small press publishing.

Presentations:

Shaw Stuart, sculptor

Bill Buschel, Greek storyteller, reading of stories from Greek history and myth

The Urban Artist, Japanese calligraphy lecture and demonstration

Catherine Edie, emcee, and the Connecticut Slam Poets

Sonal Vora, Odissi Indian dance performance

Ralph Nazareth, editor/publisher, Yuganta and Turn of River Press

Mario Susko, Croatian American poet, reading

Inti-Andino, Peruvian music group performance

LOCATION OF PROGRAMS

Greenwich Library

TARGET AUDIENCE

Families, teens, young adults, seniors, artists.

ATTENDANCE

3,921

MARKETING AND PUBLICITY METHODS

Greenwich Times (local daily newspaper), web page, PSAs, calendar listings, flyers mailed town-wide and distributed, interview on local public radio, monthly newsletter.

BUDGET

$8,861 ($2,000 LIVE! grant)

Frankenstein: Penetrating the Secrets of Nature

Kansas City (Mo.) Public Library

COLLABORATING ORGANIZATIONS

Not specified.

SIZE OF LIBRARY SERVICE AREA

239,525

DESCRIPTION OF PROGRAMS

Kansas City Public Library focused primarily on exhibit-related programs for adults, although the library presented a Monster Carnival aimed at young adults and story times at all facilities for young children. All of the programs were planned and implemented by the specially created Frankie's Team—a staff program committee under the direction of the adult program supervisor.

FORMAT AND PRESENTERS

Grand Opening: Mary Shelley Speaks—reception, self-guided exhibit tours, and chautauqua presentation—Susan Frontczak, Denver historian and actress.

Book discussion series on ethical and social challenges brought about by scientific innovation: *Frankenstein: The Modern Prometheus*, by Mary Shelley; *Dr. Jekyll and Mr. Hyde*, by Robert Louis Stevenson; *Do Androids Dream of Electric Sheep?* by Philip K. Dick; *Mendel's Dwarf*, by Simon Mawer—Alan Lubert, facilitator.

Monster Carnival—children's fair and festival with screening of *Monsters, Inc.*, face painting, races and games, and meeting costumed characters—librarians and characters.

Film discussion series—screening and facilitated discussion of *Bride of Frankenstein*, *Frankenstein's Daughter*, *Young Frankenstein*, *Rocky Horror Picture Show*, *Elephant Man*, and *Gods and Monsters*—Bob Lunn, facilitator.

Designer Genes: Health Care and the Future—lecture and discussion on the impact of scientific advancement on the value systems of medical care consumers and providers—Alan Lubert, social ethicist, facilitator.

Kansas City Haunts—reception and trolley tour of ghostly Kansas City locations—Barbara Magerl, historian and guide.

Blood drive—mobile unit accepts donations—Community Blood Center of Kansas City. (Publicity urged Kansas Citians to take creating life into their own hands and donate a pint of blood. Information about bone marrow registry and organ donation was available.)

Lisa Hefner Heitz: Ghost Stories—author presentation and book signing—Lisa Hefner Heitz, author of *Haunted Kansas*.

Chuck Palahniuk: Author Presentation—author talk and book signing held off-site in partnership with a local bookstore; exploration of Mary Shelley's themes of otherness, deformity, and artistic freedom—Chuck Palahniuk.

Children's story times—reading to small children of themed selections such as *A Monster Is Coming, A Monster Is Coming*, by Florence Heide, and *Go Away, Big Green Monster*, by Ed Emberley; children made monster paper bag puppets—children's librarians.

University tie-in—Rockhurst University chose *Frankenstein* as the freshman class all-campus read during the first two weeks of September.

LOCATION OF PROGRAMS

Main Library

TARGET AUDIENCE

Adults, children, teens, and people from throughout the metropolitan Kansas City area who are interested in the Frankenstein traveling exhibit and programs that explore the nature of life, death, and individual responsibility.

ATTENDANCE

Library attendance during exhibition period:
  38,001
Program attendance: 1,972

MARKETING AND PUBLICITY METHODS

Brochure/mailer, bookmark, Monster Carnival poster, Mary Shelley Speaks invitation, press release to calendar groups, general media mailing, e-mail promotion; target *Kansas City Star* sections and writers with specific programs.

BUDGET

Actual expenses: $9,875.40
In-kind: $11,960

Voices from the Rim

King County Library System, Issaquah, Wash.

COLLABORATING ORGANIZATION

Uwajimaya Inc.

SIZE OF LIBRARY SERVICE AREA

1,090,968

DESCRIPTION OF PROGRAMS

September 15–30, 2001: program series aimed at expanding awareness of Asian/Pacific Rim culture and the way immigration from those countries has effected change in King County.

FORMAT AND PRESENTERS

Twenty-four author events and fifty cultural events, kicked off by the Voices from the Rim Festival, Saturday, September 15, 2001.

Readers and Performers:

Seattle International Lion Dance Team (China)

Kaze Daiko—taiko drum group (Japan)

Amauta—music from the Andes (South America)

Ha Jin (China)

Molly Gloss (Pacific Northwest)

Brenda Peterson (Pacific Northwest)

Linda Minatoya (Pacific Northwest and Japan)

Philip Red Eagle (Pacific Coast Native American and Vietnam)

Lensey Namioka (China and Japan)

Janet Wong (Pacific Northwest and Korea)

Alan Chong Lau (Pacific Northwest)

David James Duncan (United States)

Plus eight other cultural/artisan/craft programs

LOCATION OF PROGRAMS

Festival kickoff: Bellevue Regional Library

Other: various community library sites and Kirkland Performance Center

TARGET AUDIENCE

Asian and Pacific Island populations, students, general public.

ATTENDANCE

3,479 (week following September 11, 2001)

MARKETING AND PUBLICITY METHODS

This large library system has all of the best promotional methods in place. Their promotion included website link and feature graphics; full-color poster; brochure mailer; program booklets; newsletter coverage; magazine coverage; PSAs; press releases, e-mails; calendar listing placement; PR newswire release; phone pitches to dailies, weeklies, and regional monthlies; paid advertising in Seattle weekly and regional papers; paid radio ads; outdoor media advertising via King County Library System trucks and King County Metro buses.

BUDGET

$60,500 ($3,000 LIVE! grant)

Let Freedom Ring! September 11:
Maine Communities Read and Reflect

Maine Libraries

COLLABORATING ORGANIZATIONS

Maine Humanities Council and sixty-three libraries, with assistance from the Maine State Library and Study Circle Resource Center, a project of the Topsfield Foundation.

SIZE OF LIBRARY SERVICE AREA

Not specified. (Population of Maine is 1.3 million.)

DESCRIPTION OF PROGRAMS

One month after the events of September 11, 2001, citizens throughout Maine gathered in their local libraries to share their thoughts about that tragic day and its consequences. Participants read excerpts from Franklin D. Roosevelt's Four Freedoms speech and W. H. Auden's poem "September 1, 1939," along with a short piece of historical background on the readings.

FORMAT AND PRESENTERS

Discussion programs were held simultaneously in libraries throughout the state on Thursday, October, 11, 2001, 7:00 to 8:30 p.m. Discussions were led by scholars and other experienced facilitators, using a single set of guidelines for all sites that was available on the Maine Humanities Council website.

LOCATION OF PROGRAMS

Local public libraries throughout the state.

TARGET AUDIENCE

Not specified.

ATTENDANCE

More than one thousand Mainers took part in this evening of reading and reflection at sixty-three libraries throughout Maine.

MARKETING AND PUBLICITY METHODS

Materials distributed entirely via website.

BUDGET

Not specified.

The Jazz Age in Paris:
1914–1940

Missoula (Mont.) Public Library

COLLABORATING ORGANIZATIONS

University of Montana Libraries, Smithsonian Institution Traveling Exhibition Service (SITES).

SIZE OF LIBRARY SERVICE AREA

95,802

DESCRIPTION OF PROGRAMS

To support a traveling exhibition from the American Library Association and the Smithsonian Institution Traveling Exhibition Service, the Missoula Public Library presented an unusually large number of well-attended programs throughout the community, including lectures, concerts, drama, radio programs, and related exhibits. All lectures were audio- or videotaped and have been added to the University of Montana Instructional Media Services collection.

FORMAT AND PRESENTERS

Jazz as a Metaphor for Democracy—pre-exhibit opening lecture at the University of Montana—Dr. Billy Taylor (800 attendance).

Afternoon jazz seminar—Dr. Taylor (200 attendance).

Jazz concert—Billy Taylor Trio (750 attendance).

Opening reception at library featuring ragtime piano and exhibit video.

Lecture series on topics including Hemingway's Paris; Jazz in Francophone Literature; Life of Django Reinhardt; Jazz-Age Dance; Jazz Age in America; Stein, Picasso, Louis Armstrong; Life of Sidney Bechet; Jazz and Blues Motifs in Sartre's *La Nausée*; New Perceptions, New Paradigms; Jazz and the Cinematographic New Wave; and Paris and Food—presenters were scholars from the University of Montana and New York University, including Drs. William Bevis, Gerry Brenner, Sylvie Kande, William Knowles, Michael Mayer, Chris Anderson, Michael Valentin, and Gary Kerr.

Two jazz-related exhibits—presented by the University of Montana Museum of Fine Arts during the exhibition period (5,000 visitors).

Two youth concerts featuring Gershwin's *An American in Paris*—Missoula Symphony Orchestra (1,800 fourth graders attended).

Harlem to Paris—a Sunday afternoon jazz program focusing on the Jazz Age, presented by KUFM-Montana Public Radio during the entire exhibition period.

Jazz concerts—presented by the University of Montana jazz bands, a jazz saxophone quartet from Calgary, and the Missoula County high school jazz bands at the public library and the university during the display period.

An Evening of Stories by Ernest Hemingway—Montana Repertory Theater (472 attendance).

Exhibit highlighting the local community during the Jazz Age—the Historical Museum at Fort Missoula (900 attendance, one-third of them children).

LOCATION OF PROGRAMS

Nine lectures at the public library, one at the university. Others as indicated above. Billy Taylor events at university.

TARGET AUDIENCE

Young Audiences of Western Montana, which reaches school children throughout the twenty-county region, including Hmong, Native American, Soviet-bloc immigrants, and fifteen hundred students in Title I schools that serve economically disadvantaged populations.

ATTENDANCE

Exhibitions attendance: 16,000

Program attendance: 1,414 at thirteen lecture programs

Other attendance figures included with descriptions above.

MARKETING AND PUBLICITY METHODS

Extensive regional publicity campaign included newspaper ads, radio announcements, TV spots, mention in newsletters, and press releases to a wide range of organizations throughout the city and the university community. Local public radio station KUFM promoted the programs and exhibit very heavily and created musical programming on the station to complement the exhibit. Both the public library and the university library created bibliographies for adults' and children's materials. The university bibliography was distributed on campus, at local bookstores, and at all programs. It was also posted on the university library website. Evaluation forms distributed at programs indicated that half the audience had not attended library programs previously. Twelve percent of people signing a guest book were from outside the Missoula area.

BUDGET

$22,929 outright; $4,371 in-kind from Montana Committee for the Humanities, University of Montana President's Lecture Series, University of Montana Excellence Fund, KUFM public radio, Friends of the Mansfield Library, Missoula Public Library Foundation, Friends of the Missoula Public Library, UM Productions, Holiday Inn Parkside, Budget Travel.

The Great Experiment:
George Washington and the American Republic

Loudonville (Ohio) Public Library

COLLABORATING ORGANIZATIONS

Ohio Humanities Council, Loudonville Boy Scouts, Huntington Library.

SIZE OF LIBRARY SERVICE AREA

10,000

DESCRIPTION OF PROGRAMS

The library hosted a series of twelve programs and additional activities, promotions, and events to coincide with the ALA traveling exhibition on George Washington.

FORMAT AND PRESENTERS

Opening ceremony and reception—Ken Hammontree.

George Washington Story Celebration—story time—Laura Lee Wilson.

Mt. Vernon in Pictures—slide presentation—Colleen Sandusky.

The Supreme Court and Public Policy under George Washington—lecture—Dr. Sherman Jackson.

Presentation at Rotary luncheon—Gayle Patton.

George Washington Family Reading Night—interactive multimedia presentation—Laura Lee Wilson.

Heirloom Plants—discussion—Charles Applegate of Kingwood Center.

George Washington Story/Craft—tour by Laura Lee Wilson and Colleen Sandusky.

Meet George Washington—first-person presentation—Ken Hammontree.

Multimedia presentation at George Washington High School —Colleen Sandusky.

Story time at Loudonville Training Center (off-site) —Laura Lee Wilson.

Coloring contest for kindergarteners and first graders.

Illustration contest for pupils in second through sixth grades.

Essay contest for middle-school students.

Essay contest for high-school students.

Visits to the exhibition by classes and schools and curriculum materials distributed to schools.

LOCATION OF PROGRAMS

Mainly on-site

TARGET AUDIENCE

Not specified.

ATTENDANCE

Gate count: 15,215; estimate of exhibit visitors: 2,093

Programs: 144 adults, 43 young adults, 380 children, 943 schoolchildren

MARKETING AND PUBLICITY METHODS

News releases and articles in local papers, flyers, websites, contests, personal appearances, work through local schools, civic groups, colleges, and humanities organizations.

BUDGET

$780 raised from outside sources in addition to exhibit from ALA and library expenses.

Listening to the Prairie

Oklahoma State University Library

COLLABORATING ORGANIZATIONS

Smithsonian Institution's National Museum of Natural History, U.S. Department of Agriculture.

SIZE OF LIBRARY SERVICE AREA

The Stillwater campus enrolls 22,000 students and has approximately 1,100 full-time equivalent faculty and staff. In addition to serving students, faculty, and staff, the library, as a land-grant institution, serves the statewide community of 3 million Oklahoma residents.

DESCRIPTION OF PROGRAMS

A wide range of programs with appeal to the university community as well as to the community at large to accompany the American Library Association traveling exhibition.

FORMAT AND PRESENTERS

Sneak preview reception for library employees and friends of the OSU Library board of directors.

Symposium and opening reception.

Overlooked Beauty: Grasses and Grasslands—brown bag luncheon slide/lecture presentation—Dr. Ron Tyrl, professor of botany, Oklahoma State University.

Connect with the Prairie—program for junior Girl Scouts (grades 4 through 6) from the Magic Empire Council of Girl Scouts—library staff, the OSU Botanical Society, and Eco-OSU.

Hands-on Science Activities at the Black Mesa Ecological Academy—brown bag luncheon

slide/lecture presentation—Greg Federko, student at Stillwater High School and participant in Black Mesa Ecological Academy; Mark Moseley, Natural Resources Conservation Service; and Dr. Christine Moseley, associate professor, School of Leadership Studies, Oklahoma State University.

The Great Plains: A Romance of the Landscape—slide/lecture presentation—Dr. Tom Isern, professor of history, North Dakota State University.

Wheat Weaving—brown bag luncheon slide/lecture presentation—Lynn Rohrs, Wichita Wheat Weavers Guild.

Man and the Grasses: An Intimate Affair—brown bag luncheon slide/lecture presentation—Dr. Ron Tyrl, professor of botany, Oklahoma State University.

LOCATION OF PROGRAMS

Library Browsing Room

TARGET AUDIENCE

All programs were targeted to the general public, except for the Girl Scout workshop targeted to girls in grades four through six and their leaders.

ATTENDANCE

Exhibit visitors: 12,961

Total library visitors during exhibit period: 187,382

Program attendance: 741

MARKETING AND PUBLICITY METHODS

Website, outreach to groups, program flyers, customized brochures, invitations to special events, campus newsletters, public service announcements on public radio, daily newspaper.

BUDGET

Losing Geography, Discovering Self

Free Library of Philadelphia

Actual and in-kind: $21,225; supported by Division of Agricultural and Natural Resources, Oklahoma State University Library; Friends of the Oklahoma State University Library; Wal-Mart.

COLLABORATING ORGANIZATIONS

Each library hosting a performance set up partnering relationships with appropriate community groups (such as the Neuman Senior Center, Marlo Book Store, Germantown Historical Society).

SIZE OF LIBRARY SERVICE AREA

1.5 million

DESCRIPTION OF PROGRAMS

April 21 to May 9: Three authors present free lectures, readings, or book discussions to the public. The immigrant experiences and literary work of these highly regarded authors closely mirrors the personal histories of residents in Philadelphia's ethnic neighborhoods. Presentations by the authors will stress the value of cultural pride and ethnic identity. The public will be encouraged to read the works of the authors and examine and discuss their own experiences.

FORMAT AND PRESENTERS

Lectures and discussions by Ken Kalfus, Naomi Shihab Nye, and Craig Lesley.

Writing workshops, lectures, and book discussions by Ilene Renshaw, Nora Faynberg, and Igor Kaplan.

LOCATION OF PROGRAMS

Central Library, Northeast Regional Library, Northwest Regional Library, David Neuman Senior Center.

TARGET AUDIENCE

Teens, seniors, immigrant groups, general public.

ATTENDANCE

884

MARKETING AND PUBLICITY METHODS

PSAs, bilingual press releases, calendar listings, bilingual flyers and bookmarks, pitching to Russian press as well as English-speaking press, distribution of promotional pieces through partner organizations, distribution at programs of book lists that also promote future programs.

BUDGET

$14,088 ($2,250 LIVE! grant)

REFERENCES

This list includes works both specifically cited in the text and those that were consulted while the book was in formation.

American Library Association Public Information Office. 1987. *PR primer*. Chicago: American Library Association.

American Library Association Public Programs Office (ALA/PPO). 1994. *The whole person catalog 3: The source for information about arts and humanities programming in libraries*. Ed. Susan Brandehoff. Chicago: American Library Association.

———. 1998. *LIVE! @ the library: Workshop notebook*. Chicago: American Library Association Public Programs Office.

———. 1999a. *Cultural programs for adults in public libraries: A survey report*. Prepared by Debra Wilcox Johnson. Chicago: American Library Association Public Programs Office.

———. 1999b. *Let's talk about it* tip sheet. Chicago: American Library Association Public Programs Office.

Brandehoff, Susan. 1997. Turning libraries into cultural centers. *American Libraries* (March): 41–43.

———. 2003. The Frankenstein allure. *American Libraries* (December).

Candy, Philip C. 1991. *Self-direction for lifelong learning: A comprehensive guide to theory and practice*. San Francisco: Jossey-Bass.

de la Peña McCook, Kathleen. 2000a. *A place at the table: Participating in community building*. Chicago: American Library Association.

———. 2000b. Librarians and comprehensive community initiatives. *Reference and User Services Quarterly* 40 (Fall): 24–31.

———. 2001. Authentic discourse as a means of connection between public library service responses and community-building initiatives. *Reference and User Services Quarterly* 41 (Winter): 127–33.

Geever, Jane C., and Patricia McNeill. 1997. *The Foundation Center's guide to proposal writing*, rev. ed. New York: Foundation Center.

Hayes, Laura. 2002. Coping, view 1: Programs laudable. *American Libraries* (September): 35.

Heim, Kathleen M., and Danny P. Wallace, eds. 1990. *Adult services: An enduring focus for public libraries.* Chicago: American Library Association.

Lear, Brett W. 2002. *Adult programs in the library.* Chicago: American Library Association.

McCarthy, Kevin F., and Kimberly Jinnett. 2001. *A new framework for building participation in the arts.* Santa Monica, CA: Rand.

Miller, Berna. 1997. The quest for lifelong learning. *American Demographics* (March): 20–22.

Miner, Lynn E., et al. 1998. *Proposal planning and writing,* 2nd ed. Phoenix: Oryx Press.

Monroe, Margaret E. 1981. The cultural role of the public library. In vol. 11 of *Advances in librarianship,* ed. Michael H. Harris. New York: Academic Press.

Moores, Alan, and Rhea Rubin. 1984. *Let's talk about it: A planner's manual.* Chicago: American Library Association.

National Endowment for the Arts. 1998. *1997 survey of public participation in the arts.* NEA Research Division report no. 39. Washington, DC: National Endowment for the Arts.

Outcome evaluation toolkit: How libraries and librarians help. Project Directors: Joan C. Durrance and Karen Pettigrew-Fisher. (http://ibec.ischool.washington.edu/ibecCat.aspx?subCat=Outcome%20Toolkit&cat=Tools%20and%20Resources)

Putnam, Robert D. 2000. *Bowling alone: The collapse and revival of American community.* New York: Simon and Schuster.

Quick, Sam, et al. 1984. Sharing our selves: A basis for lifelong learning. *The Futurist* (June): 20–22.

Rifkin, Jeremy. 1995. *The end of work: The decline of the global labor force and the dawn of the post-market era.* New York: Putnam.

———. 2000. *The age of access: The new culture of hypercapitalism where all of life is a paid-for experience.* New York: Penguin/Putnam.

Robertson, Deb. 2002. Oprah and out: Libraries keep book clubs flourishing. *American Libraries* (September): 52–53.

Rubin, Rhea Joyce. 1997. *Humanities programming: A how-to-do-it manual.* How-to-do-it manuals for librarians, no. 72. New York: Neal-Schuman.

Van Fleet, Connie, and Douglas Raber. 1990. The public library as a social/cultural institution: Alternative perspectives and changing contexts. In *Adult services: An enduring focus for public libraries,* ed. Kathleen M. Heim and Danny P. Wallace, 456–500. Chicago: American Library Association.

Wallace, Danny P. 1990. The character of adult services in the eighties: Overview and analysis of the ASE questionnaire data. In

Adult services: An enduring focus for public libraries, ed. Kathleen M. Heim and Danny P. Wallace, 27–165. Chicago: American Library Association.

Wiegand, Wayne A. 2003. To reposition a research agenda: What American studies can teach the LIS community about the library in the life of the user. *Library Quarterly* 73 (4): 369–82.

Page numbers in bold refer to worksheets and forms. Page numbers in italics refer to samples and illustrations.

DEBORAH A. ROBERTSON is director of the Public Programs Office of the American Library Association, an office she established in 1990. Since then, its audience has grown to an estimated ten million participants. Robertson has created more than twenty nationwide programs and initiatives, including traveling exhibitions, reading and discussion program series, and literary and cultural programming. She has served as an adviser on library projects to such organizations as the Smithsonian Institution, PBS, the Poetry Foundation, YMCA National Writer's Voice, and Brown University. She is a popular ALA speaker at national, division, and state library association conferences.

DEMCO